THE WORDS
OF *Jesus*

Publications International, Ltd.

Let's get social!

 @Publications_International

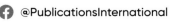 @PublicationsInternational

www.pilbooks.com

Table of Contents

Introduction

It can be difficult to make the right decisions sometimes, to strive to be the better person when the world around you seems increasingly more detached and self-absorbed. Take comfort in your faith and look around you with an open heart. *The Words of Jesus* is a daily guide to help broaden your devotion as you reflect on Jesus' teachings of love, mercy, and forgiveness.

Throughout this book, you'll find verses, reflections, and prayers for every day of the calendar year. Spending time with the teachings of Jesus will help you discover the many ways his love appears in your life, even on difficult days. With him by your side, you will never walk alone.

January

> Verily, verily, I say unto you, That ye shall
> weep and lament, but the world shall rejoice:
> and ye shall be sorrowful, but your sorrow shall
> be turned into joy.
>
> —John 16:20

The slate is clean, Lord, the calendar as bare as the Christmas tree. Bless the New Year that beckons. Help us face what we must, celebrate every triumph we can, and make any changes we need. We're celebrating to the fullest this whistle-blowing, toast-raising moment, for it is the threshold between the old and new in us.

January 2

> **Behold, I make all things new.**
>
> **—Revelation 21:5**

O Lord, the best thing about the New Year is the word new! All the resolutions I make are meaningless unless I am truly new from the inside out. Give me a new attitude, Lord! A new focus, a new passion, a new mission—all based on the new things you want to do through me this year.

Thou shalt not tempt the Lord thy God.

—Luke 4:12

All our opportunities, abilities, and resources come from God. They are given to us to hold in sacred trust for him. Cooperating with God will permit us to generously pass on to others some of the many blessings from his rich storehouse.

> And there came a leper to him, beseeching
> him, and kneeling down to him, and saying unto
> him, If thou wilt, thou canst make me clean.
> And Jesus, moved with compassion, put forth his
> hand, and touched him, and saith unto him,
> I will; be thou clean.
>
> —Mark 1:40–41

There is no problem too big for God to help us with
it, no wound or hurt too deep for healing. Cleanse us,
Lord, of all that hurts us and hinders us emotionally,
spiritually, and physically.

> Take therefore no thought for the morrow:
> for the morrow shall take thought for
> the things of itself. Sufficient unto the day is
> the evil thereof.
>
> —Matthew 6:34

The past, O God of yesterdays, todays, and promise-filled tomorrows, can be an anchor or a launching pad. It's sometimes so easy to look back on the pain and hurt and believe the future may be an instant replay. Help us to accept the aches of the past and put them in perspective so we can also see the many ways you supported and nurtured us. Then, believing in your promise of regeneration, launch us into the future free and excited to live in joy.

No man also seweth a piece of new cloth on an old garment: else the new piece that filled it up taketh away from the old, and the rent is made worse. And no man putteth new wine into old bottles: else the new wine doth burst the bottles, and the wine is spilled, and the bottles will be marred: but new wine must be put into new bottles.

—Mark 2:21-22

Lord, thank you for being a God of new beginnings. Give me a fresh start today as I trust in you. Amen.

> **Ye are the light of the world. A city that is set on an hill cannot be hid.**
>
> —Matthew 5:14

Some people seem to radiate God's light to others. Their love for God and for others spills over in everything they do. I ask your blessing today on those who work to spread God's light—especially pastors, teachers, Bible study and prayer group leaders, and chaplains.

> Whosoever therefore shall break one of these least commandments, and shall teach men so, he shall be called the least in the kingdom of heaven: but whosoever shall do and teach them, the same shall be called great in the kingdom of heaven.
>
> —Matthew 5:19

We all want to do something effective in this world while we are here. The key is being faithful to what God lays on our heart.

> And ye now therefore have sorrow: but I will see you again, and your heart shall rejoice, and your joy no man taketh from you.
>
> —John 16:22

Renewal in the Lord has brought us unspeakable joy.

> Therefore if thou bring thy gift to the altar,
> and there rememberest that thy brother hath
> ought against thee; Leave there thy gift before the
> altar, and go thy way; first be reconciled to thy
> brother, and then come and offer thy gift.
>
> —Matthew 5:23-24

I need to ask someone for forgiveness. Part of me wants to brush off and minimize what I did, to say that what I did wasn't so bad—maybe the other person didn't even notice! But I don't want to start to walk astray in little things. God, give me strength to do this properly and offer a genuine, loving apology.

Swear not at all; neither by heaven; for it
is God's throne: Nor by the earth; for it is his
footstool: neither by Jerusalem; for it is the city
of the great King. Neither shalt thou swear by
thy head, because thou canst not make one hair
white or black. But let your communication be,
Yea, yea; Nay, nay: for whatsoever is more than
these cometh of evil.

—Matthew 5:34-37

When we think of integrity, we
think of someone who is honorable
and trustworthy—a person who
keeps their word and guards their
reputation. Jesus provides the best
example of a man of integrity. He was
not swayed by outer influences but
lived a life above reproach. Integrity
comes not just from the pursuit of
right living, but the pursuit of God,
which leads to right living.

> He that received the seed into stony places, the same is he that heareth the word, and anon with joy receiveth it.
>
> **—Matthew 13:20**

Lord, you are the source of all joy! Regardless of how happy we may feel at any given time, we know happiness is fleeting. Happiness, so dependent on temporary circumstances, is fickle and unpredictable. But joy in you is forever! And so we come to you today, Lord, rejoicing in all you were, all you are, and all you will ever be. Because of you, we rejoice!

> Forgive, if ye have ought against any:
> that your Father also which is in heaven may
> forgive you your trespasses.
>
> —Mark 11:25

Lord God, the words "I'm sorry" and "forgive me" have got to be the most powerful in our vocabulary. May these phrases ever be poised on my lips, ready to do their work of release and restoration. Let your healing balm wash over me, Father, as I both grant and receive the freedom that forgiveness brings. Amen.

> The glory which thou gavest me I have given them; that they may be one, even as we are one: I in them, and thou in me, that they may be made perfect in one; and that the world may know that thou hast sent me, and hast loved them, as thou hast loved me.
>
> —John 17:22-23

God, your blessings abound. Even in the dark of winter, I see your hand in the beauty of frost on the windowpane, the kindness of the grocery clerk who helps an elderly woman load her purchases in her car, and the diligence of those who work at night to clear the roads. Even though it gets dark early these days, I see your light shining.

Bless are ye that weep now: for ye shall laugh.

—Luke 6:21

There are many events in our lives over which we have no control. However, we do have a choice either to endure trying times and press on or to give up. The secret of survival, whether or not we question God's presence or his ability to help us, is remembering that our hope is in the fairness, goodness, and justice of God. When we put our trust in the character of a God who cannot fail us, we will remain faithful. Our trust and faithfulness produce the endurance that sees us through the "tough stuff" we all face in this life.

Peace I leave with you, my peace I give unto
you: not as the world giveth, give I unto you.
Let not your heart be troubled, neither let it
be afraid.

—John 14:27

To live a life of faith is to live always in God's presence,
at peace in the home of his love.

Ask, and it shall be given you; seek, and ye shall find; knock, and it shall be opened unto you: For every one that asketh receiveth; and he that seeketh findeth; and to him that knocketh it shall be opened.

—Matthew 7:7-8

Each prayer is a message of faith in God. We are saying, "I trust you; lead me. I believe in you; guide me. I need you; show me." When we offer ourselves openly, he will always answer.

> Let your light so shine before men, that they may see your good works, and glorify your Father which is in heaven.
>
> —Matthew 5:16

God, Creator of all things, ultimately all light comes from you. I praise you and glorify you, Father God, source and giver of all good things.

I will put upon you none other burden. But that which ye have already hold fast till I come. And he that overcometh, and keepeth my works unto the end, to him will I give power over the nations: And he shall rule them with a rod of iron; as the vessels of a potter shall they be broken to shivers: even as I received of my Father.

—Revelation 2:24-27

It takes faith to go beyond what others know—to explore new ideas, to stand on our convictions that there is something more, and to trust that God has called us to discover it.

I will not leave you comfortless:
I will come to you.

—John 14:18

Sometimes it is difficult to appreciate snowy weather, but I thank God for the gift of snow days. How wonderful it is for everyone to be home, safe, and warm. On snow days, life returns to a simpler pace and the demands of schedules and responsibilities fall away. Thank you, Lord, for the beauty of the snow and the time it gives us to relax and share quiet times with our loved ones.

A woman when she is in travail hath sorrow,
because her hour is come: but as soon as she
is delivered of the child, she remembereth no
more the anguish, for joy that a man is born into
the world.

—John 16:21

Traumatic events leave a void in our souls that only
a closer relationship with God can fill. By asking
God to help us through hard times, we truly come to
understand that we are never alone and that sadness is
only a precursor to joy and pain a precursor to healing.

> **My grace is sufficient for thee: for my strength is made perfect in weakness.**
>
> —2 Corinthians 12:9

Some people blame their lack of faith on their different circumstances. Yet rough situations are often the catalyst for displays of great faith.

> Well done, good and faithful servant;
> thou hast been faithful over a few things,
> I will make thee ruler over many things:
> enter thou into the joy of thy Lord.
>
> —Matthew 25:23

Blessings, like miracles, appear only when we believe in them. Faith gives us the eyes with which to see and to believe what we see.

> **Be not afraid, but speak, and hold not thy peace: For I am with thee, and no man shall set on thee to hurt thee.**
>
> **—Acts 18:9-10**

Father, I pray today for a clear path, a strong wind at my back pushing me forward, and the courage of a lion to step into greatness. I am afraid and uncomfortable, but with you I can begin the journey of a thousand miles—with one bold step.

> Every idle word that men shall speak,
> they shall give account thereof in the day of
> judgment. For by thy words thou shalt
> be justified, and by thy words thou shalt
> be condemned.
>
> —Matthew 12:36-37

Bless me with the kind heart of a peacemaker and a
builder's sturdy hand, Lord, for these are mean-spirited,
litigious times when we tear down with words and
weapons first and ask questions later. Help me take
every opportunity to compliment, praise, and applaud
as I rebuild peace.

Write the things which thou hast seen, and the things which are, and the things which shall be hereafter; The mystery of the seven stars which thou sawest in my right hand, and the seven golden candlesticks. The seven stars are the angels of the seven churches: and the seven candlesticks which thou sawest are the seven churches.

—Revelation 1:19-20

God's angels are messengers, giving us comfort and assurance of God's presence in any shadowy valley through which we may walk. Though his presence is not visible to us, God is found in deeds of faith, courage, and love.

Now they have known that all things
whatsoever thou hast given me are of thee. For
I have given unto them the words which thou
gavest me; and they have received them, and
have known surely that I came out from thee,
and they have believed that thou didst send me.

—John 17:7-8

God gave because he is love. It was the best he had to offer. The supreme gift. The total gift. In the person of his son, he gave himself.

Therefore take no thought, saying, What shall we eat? or, What shall we drink? or, Wherewithal shall we be clothed? (For after all these things do the Gentiles seek:) for your heavenly Father knoweth that ye have need of all these things. But seek ye first the kingdom of God, and his righteousness; and all these things shall be added unto you.

—Matthew 6:31-33

God may throw us a few curves in life—we may feel hassled, troubled, anxious, or uncomfortable, and not understand why our circumstances don't fit our desires. But if we trust in the wisdom of his plan, God will provide for all our needs.

> Neither pray I for these alone, but for them also which shall believe on me through their word; That they all may be one; as thou, Father, art in me, and I in thee, that they also may be one in us: that the world may believe that thou hast sent me.
>
> —John 17:20-21

The blessing of faith in the Lord is salvation.

He that receiveth you receiveth me, and he that receiveth me receiveth him that sent me. He that receiveth a prophet in the name of a prophet shall receive a prophet's reward; and he that receiveth a righteous man in the name of a righteous man shall receive a righteous man's reward.

—Matthew 10:40-41

A dedicated servant is grateful to all those who have served him, including the Lord. He sees that he is passing on to others what he has received.

> **I have glorified thee on the earth: I have finished the work which thou gavest me to do.**
>
> **—John 17:4**

Lord, we live in a world where there is a great clamoring for power and glory. Greed runs rampant, and time and time again we see the inglorious results of someone's unethical attempts to climb to the top. Protect us from such fruitless ambition, Lord. For we know that it is only when we humble ourselves that you will lift us up higher than we could ever have imagined. All power and glory is yours, forever and ever. Until we acknowledge that truth, we will never be great in anyone's eyes—especially yours.

February

> **He that overcometh shall inherit all things;**
> **and I will be his God, and he shall be my son.**
>
> **—Revelation 21:7**

Well, it's a new month. We're in the dregs of winter, though, and it's hard to feel fresh and new. It's been gray and dreary outside, and the kids are bored and restless, tired of school and eager for spring sports to begin again.

Lord, I know you take us where we're at. Please give me the grace to see the blessings in the ordinary and humdrum. Thank you for the crises that aren't happening, the text from a friend with a funny joke, my spouse taking the car in for an oil change. Bless my family, and my friends, and the service workers I meet as I run my errands.

> He arose, and rebuked the wind, and said
> unto the sea, Peace, be still. And the wind
> ceased, and there was a great calm. And he said
> unto them, Why are ye so fearful? how is it that
> ye have no faith?
>
> —Mark 4:39-40

Why tornadoes, Lord? Why typhoons or fires? Why floods or earthquakes? Why devastating accidents or acts of terror, Lord? It's so hard to understand. Perhaps there is no way to find any sense in overwhelming circumstances. Perhaps it's about trusting in you, God, no matter what comes and leaving it in your hands, where it belongs because, in fact, you do really love us and care about us and will make things work out for us.

Ye have heard that it hath been said, Thou shalt love thy neighbour, and hate thine enemy. But I say unto you, Love your enemies, bless them that curse you, do good to them that hate you, and pray for them which despitefully use you, and persecute you; That ye may be the children of your Father which is in heaven: for he maketh his sun to rise on the evil and on the good, and sendeth rain on the just and on the unjust.

—Matthew 5:43-45

When we see our enemies from God's perspective, compassion follows, for he has seen the sorrows in their hearts that have caused them to behave in such a manner. He longs to reach out to these people and comfort them, and he sometimes uses our hands to do it.

February 4

> He answereth him, and saith, O faithless
> generation, how long shall I be with you? how
> long shall I suffer you?
>
> —Mark 9:19

Lord, help me trust you enough to tear down the walls
of fear and doubt.

> Suffer the little children to come unto me, and forbid them not: for of such is the kingdom of God. Verily I say unto you, Whosoever shall not receive the kingdom of God as a little child, he shall not enter therein.
>
> —Mark 10:14-15

Dear God, thank you for children who teach us to be open and forgiving. Help us forgive those who hurt us so the pain will not be passed on through the generations. Thank you for forgiving our sins and help us be at peace with our families. Amen.

February 6

> **And he began to say unto them, This day is this scripture fulfilled in your ears.**
>
> **—Luke 4:21**

Lord, focusing on your Word is a great blessing. The more I keep it before me, the more faithfully I walk in your ways. Help me to make the most of every opportunity I have to read, think about, and discuss the things you share with us through the Scriptures. Give me a fresh start today as I trust in you. Amen.

And he said unto them, In what place soever ye enter into an house, there abide till ye depart from that place. And whosoever shall not receive you, nor hear you, when ye depart thence, shake off the dust under your feet for a testimony against them. Verily I say unto you, It shall be more tolerable for Sodom and Gomorrha in the day of judgment, than for that city.

—Mark 6:10-11

Whether we admit it or not, we all long to feel welcomed and accepted by others. Just as Jesus connected with people outside his circle of disciples, we need to connect with people outside our comfort zone and mirror God's acceptance of all people.

Ye are the salt of the earth.

—Matthew 5:13

Salt gives flavor and taste. As Christians, we are called to bring God's joy, love, and comfort to others. Salt also preserves, and we are also called to hold to the truth against corruption.

> Verily I say unto you, All sins shall be
> forgiven unto the sons of men, and blasphemies
> wherewith soever they shall blaspheme:
> But he that shall blaspheme against the Holy
> Ghost hath never forgiveness, but is in
> danger of eternal damnation.
>
> —Mark 3:28-29

Lord, it's hard for me to conceive of how thoroughly you forgive me when I confess my sins to you. The stains on my soul are washed away, and you give me a fresh, clean start. Even though it's hard for me to wrap my understanding around this, please help me wrap my faith around it so I can believe that you completely forgive me.

> **Blessed are they which do hunger and thirst after righteousness: for they shall be filled.**
>
> —Matthew 5:6

There's so much injustice in this world. There are so many people hurting because of other people's carelessness, selfishness, or desire for power and wealth at other people's expense. Please grant me a giving, generous heart when it comes to treating people fairly, to taking care of the widow and orphan, and to acting justly. When it becomes overwhelming, please help me discern where my efforts can do the most good in righting wrongs in my social circles and my community.

He that hath an ear, let him hear what the
Spirit saith unto the churches;
He that overcometh shall not be hurt of
the second death.

—Revelation 2:11

A strong spirit can overcome even the weakest flesh.

> And unto him that smiteth thee on the one cheek offer also the other; and him that taketh away thy cloke forbid not to take thy coat also. Give to every man that asketh of thee; and of him that taketh away thy goods ask them not again. And as ye would that men should do to you, do ye also to them likewise.
>
> —Luke 6:29-31

God stretches our heart's capacity when he tells us to love our enemies. Loving them proves that we belong to God, for he loves everyone, no matter what they have done.

Go home to thy friends, and tell them how
great things the Lord hath done for thee, and
hath had compassion on thee.

—Mark 5:19

Lord, give me your compassion today. When I look at
the people around me, help me to see them through
your eyes. I know you love us all equally, Lord. And
you love us completely and unconditionally. May I
compassionately reach out to others in your name today.

February 14

> A new commandment I give unto you, That ye love one another; as I have loved you, that ye also love one another. By this shall all men know that ye are my disciples, if ye have love one to another.
>
> —John 13:34-35

It's Valentine's Day! While this holiday can be commercial, let me take it as an opportunity to thank you, God, for the people I love and the people who love me. I know all love ultimately flows from you, for you are love.

> He that hath my commandments, and
> keepeth them, he it is that loveth me: and he
> that loveth me shall be loved of my Father, and I
> will love him, and will manifest myself to him.
>
> —John 14:21

If God has touched us with his love, the result will be love flowing through us to others. When we realize the depth of his love, our hearts long to show that kind of love to those around us.

February 16

> The kingdom of heaven is like unto treasure
> hid in a field; the which when a man hath found,
> he hideth, and for joy thereof goeth and selleth
> all that he hath, and buyeth that field.
>
> **—Matthew 13:44**

O God, giver of all good things, our faith in you is like a treasure to be mined—it sustains, it inspires, and it provides us with unimagined contentment.

> Hearken unto me every one of you, and understand: There is nothing from without a man, that entering into him can defile him: but the things which come out of him, those are they that defile the man. If any man have ears to hear, let him hear.
>
> —Mark 7:14-16

Forgive us, Lord, our sins, for failing to live up to your standards of goodness and justice. We confess our shortcomings to you. Make us willing to change and help us become persons of godly character. Amen.

And he said unto them, This kind can come forth by nothing, but by prayer and fasting.

—Mark 9:29

Our faith can only thrive if we stay focused on God rather than on ourselves.

> But love ye your enemies, and do good, and lend, hoping for nothing again; and your reward shall be great, and ye shall be the children of the Highest: for he is kind unto the unthankful and to the evil. Be ye therefore merciful, as your Father also is merciful.
>
> —Luke 6:35-36

Heavenly Father, give us the forgiving spirit we so badly need to heal the wounds of the past. Help us live "the better life" by making peace with our enemies and understanding that they, too, need your love. Let me extend your mercy to others. Amen.

> **But Jesus said unto her, Let the children first be filled: for it is not meet to take the children's bread, and to cast it unto the dogs.**
>
> **—Mark 7:27**

God, give me the patience to take this thing called life one step at a time. Stop me from rushing things and demanding they happen in my time. Give me the wisdom to allow them to happen on your clock, not mine. Amen.

Watch and pray, that ye enter not into
temptation: the spirit indeed is willing, but the
flesh is weak.

—Matthew 26:41

Give me strength today to stand against temptation.
Empower me with the faith that I can say no to things
that don't add to my peace or happiness without guilt
or regret. Give me, God, the courage to turn away from
things that might bring fleeting pleasure, but may not be
your will for me. I ask today in prayer for the strength to
do what is right, what is just, and what is fair, even if I
am tempted to cheat, lie, or take more than my fair share.

Thou shalt love the Lord thy God with all thy heart, and with all thy soul, and with all thy mind, and with all thy strength: this is the first commandment.

—Mark 12:30

Faith in God's love frees me to be the real me, for I remember that God sees me as I am and loves me with all his heart.

> **Thou shalt love thy neighbour as thyself.**
>
> —Mark 12:31

When neighbors don't measure up to our expectations, we can go to God for a change of heart. With his example and assistance, we can love our neighbors as God wants us to.

> The kingdom of heaven is like unto a merchant man, seeking goodly pearls: Who, when he had found one pearl of great price, went and sold all that he had, and bought it.
>
> —Matthew 13:45-46

Lord, put into my heart a pure faith that is fit for the kingdom of heaven.

Take heed that ye do not your alms before men, to be seen of them: otherwise ye have no reward of your Father which is in heaven. Therefore when thou doest thine alms, do not sound a trumpet before thee, as the hypocrites do in the synagogues and in the streets, that they may have glory of men. Verily I say unto you, They have their reward. But when thou doest alms, let not thy left hand know what thy right hand doeth: That thine alms may be in secret: and thy Father which seeth in secret himself shall reward thee openly.

—Matthew 6:1-4

Beware of smugness and pride—do not let those feelings guide your actions. Instead, try to keep your thoughts and actions genuine, rather than using them to gain attention from others.

February 26

> **Blessed are they that hear the word of God,**
> **and keep it.**
>
> —Luke 11:28

God, help me become a powerful loving presence in the world. Set before me directions to the path meant for me, a path that allows me to fully express your will through my words, deeds, and actions. Amen.

> **And he said unto them, I must preach
> the kingdom of God to other cities also: for
> therefore am I sent.**
>
> —**Luke 4:43**

Having faith in God is important, but even he expects us to move our feet. Without taking action, his words of wisdom go unheeded, and his will goes unfulfilled. We best serve ourselves when we listen for his word, then move forward boldly.

> **O Father, glorify thou me with thine own self with the glory which I had with thee before the world was.**
>
> **—John 17:5**

Almighty God, do we tell you often enough how awesome you are? We stand before you in complete awe of your creation, your sovereignty, and your power. Let us never minimize the ability you have to change our reality in an instant, even when it involves moving mountains or calming storms. You, O God, are the one and only God, and we give you glory at all times.

> I have manifested thy name unto the men
> which thou gavest me out of the world: thine
> they were, and thou gavest them me; and they
> have kept thy word.
>
> —John 17:6

When you need a helping hand, look around for the angels God has placed in your path. Human angels come in the form of friends, mentors, and even strangers with words meant just for you to hear. Reach out, look, receive God's blessings through his earthly angels.

March

> **Blessed are the peacemakers: for they shall be called the children of God.**
>
> —Matthew 5:9

What does it mean to be a peacemaker? Not to overlook wrongs, or to speak soothing platitudes, but to work out conflicts by listening to God's will. Bless those who do the work of restoring relationships in accordance with God's plan.

And he turned him unto his disciples, and
said privately, Blessed are the eyes which see
the things that ye see: For I tell you, that many
prophets and kings have desired to see those
things which ye see, and have not seen them; and
to hear those things which ye hear, and have not
heard them.

—Luke 10:23-24

Give us eyes with
which to see, noses
with which to sniff,
ears with which to
hear the faintest
sound along the paths
you have set for us,
O God of Daily Joys.
Following you is a
whole experience—
body, mind, and soul.

And when Jesus knew it, he saith unto them, Why reason ye, because ye have no bread? perceive ye not yet, neither understand? have ye your heart yet hardened? Having eyes, see ye not? and having ears, hear ye not? and do ye not remember? When I brake the five loaves among five thousand, how many baskets full of fragments took ye up? They say unto him, Twelve. And when the seven among four thousand, how many baskets full of fragments took ye up? And they said, Seven. And he said unto them, How is it that ye do not understand?

—Mark 8:17-21

Sometimes not a miracle, but just believing, takes the greatest faith of all.

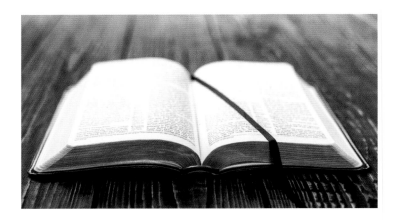

> **Man shall not live by bread alone,
> but by every Word that proceedeth out of
> the mouth of God.**
>
> **—Matthew 4:4**

Father, please instill in me a desire to seek out and delight in your holy Word. Please give me insight when I read the Scriptures, that your words illuminate my life, even when the truth is hard to hear because it demands something from me that I don't want to give.

Except a man be born of water and of the
Spirit, he cannot enter into the kingdom of God.
That which is born of the flesh is flesh; and that
which is born of the Spirit is spirit.

—John 3:5-6

Lord, how hopelessly aware we are of our earthly
bodies. They develop creaks and frailties—not to
mention weird bumps and lumps! But thanks to you,
we are so much more than our bodies. For although we
live in the flesh, we are filled with your Holy Spirit;
the life we live is really you living out your life in us!

> **See thou say nothing to any man: but go thy way, shew thyself to the priest, and offer for thy cleansing those things which Moses commanded, for a testimony unto them.**
>
> **—Mark 1:44**

Sometimes I take pride in my faith. I favorably compare my church involvement to that of others; I share a helpful spiritual practice with a friend not with humility but with an air of condescension. Lord, keep me gentle and humble of heart, aware of how reliant I am on you.

And the Father himself, which hath sent me, hath borne witness of me. Ye have neither heard his voice at any time, nor seen his shape. And ye have not his word abiding in you: for whom he hath sent, him ye believe not.

—John 5:37-38

Dear Father God, you sent your son to us to be our Lord, to watch over us, to bring us comfort, strength, hope, and healing when our hearts are broken and our lives seem shattered. We will never be alone, not when you are here with us always and forever. Remind us to look to you for strength. Amen.

March 8

Are not five sparrows sold for two farthings,
and not one of them is forgotten before God?

—Luke 12:6

Today I take joy in nature. I look around and see all that you have made. The natural world is full of your presence. Thank you for the birds migrating overhead, for the wind's breath, even for the violence of a thunderstorm. I know that everything came to be by your hand, and the world around me is a blessing.

> Jesus said unto him, If thou canst believe, all things are possible to him that believeth.
>
> —Mark 9:23

I cannot see the light, but I know it is just up ahead. I cannot find the way out, but I know that my path is leading me there. I cannot solve the problem, but I know the solution is on its way. I know these things because of my faith in God, who has never failed me, and never will.

> And he said, Take heed that ye be not
> deceived: for many shall come in my name,
> saying, I am Christ; and the time draweth near:
> go ye not therefore after them.
>
> —Luke 21:8

God, please give me a spirit of discernment, that I not stray from your Word. Not everyone who claims they are Christian preaches your truth at all times. Steer me clear of false teachings, whether they are being spread because of ignorance or ill intent.

Pilate therefore said unto him, Art thou a king then? Jesus answered, Thou sayest that I am a king. To this end was I born, and for this cause came I into the world, that I should bear witness unto the truth. Every one that is of the truth heareth my voice.

—John 18:37

Jesus fulfilled many roles during his earthly life: son, friend, teacher, and savior. He grappled with many issues—just as we do—but he patiently fulfilled the mission he came to earth to perform.

Let these sayings sink down into your ears: for the Son of man shall be delivered into the hands of men.

—Luke 9:44

Thank you for your wise ways, Lord. Following them fills my life with true blessings—the riches of love and relationship, joy and provision, peace and protection. I remember reading in your Word that whenever I ask for your wisdom from a faith-filled heart, you will give it, no holds barred. So I'll ask once again today for your insight and understanding as I build, using your blueprints.

> Abba, Father, all things are possible unto thee; take away this cup from me: nevertheless not what I will, but what thou wilt.
>
> —Mark 14:36

If our faith was never tested, how would we know we had any? When things go wrong and we can still say, "I believe in God no matter what happens," we show our faith to be real.

He that hath an ear, let him hear what the Spirit saith unto the churches; To him that overcometh will I give to eat of the hidden manna, and will give him a white stone, and in the stone a new name written, which no man knoweth saving he that receiveth it.

—Revelation 2:17

Keep God's word in your heart, and you will be rewarded.

> Woe unto you, when all men shall speak
> well of you! for so did their fathers to the
> false prophets.
>
> —Luke 6:26

Dear God, a good friend lets us know when we've
done wrong. May I be open to words of constructive
criticism, shared by those who love me; may I see false
platitudes for what they are.

Jesus answered and said unto him, If a man love me, he will keep my words: and my Father will love him, and we will come unto him, and make our abode with him. He that loveth me not keepeth not my sayings: and the word which ye hear is not mine, but the Father's which sent me.

—John 14:23-24

Lord, in your infinite wisdom you knew we would need instruction for life, and so you placed in your Word the guidelines for living a productive life that brings you glory. Your Word nurtures us body and soul and keeps our minds focused on the beautiful, positive aspects of life. Thank you, Lord, for not leaving us here without a guidebook. We'd be lost without your Word.

> Think not that I am come to destroy the law, or the prophets: I am not come to destroy, but to fulfil. For verily I say unto you, Till heaven and earth pass, one jot or one tittle shall in no wise pass from the law, till all be fulfilled.
>
> —Matthew 5:17-18

Jesus was the fulfillment of God's promise of salvation. His life and death made salvation possible for us. What a glorious, selfless gift! I ponder this blessing every day, and gratitude and joy fill my very being.

> Verily, verily, I say unto you, The servant is not greater than his lord; neither he that is sent greater than he that sent him. If ye know these things, happy are ye if ye do them.
>
> —John 13:16-17

How amazing you are, O Lord! You sent Jesus, your son, to live as one of us, to walk among us. You claim us as your own. When I am feeling downcast, let me remember that the Lord of the universe chooses to love me. Thank you and praise you!

If any man come to me, and hate not his father, and mother, and wife, and children, and brethren, and sisters, yea, and his own life also, he cannot be my disciple.

—Luke 14:26

Love God first, and all of your other relationships will fall into place.

March 20

> Whereunto shall we liken the kingdom of God? or with what comparison shall we compare it? It is like a grain of mustard seed, which, when it is sown in the earth, is less than all the seeds that be in the earth: But when it is sown, it groweth up, and becometh greater than all herbs, and shooteth out great branches; so that the fowls of the air may lodge under the shadow of it.
>
> —Mark 4:30-32

Kindness sows a seed within me that begins to sprout where before all was barren. Leaves of trust start to bud, and I branch out. I take in gentle caring and loving nudging and realize I might just go ahead and bloom! After all, God arranged spring after winter.

> Ye judge after the flesh; I judge no man. And yet if I judge, my judgment is true: for I am not alone, but I and the Father that sent me.
>
> —John 8:15-16

Jesus, who will one day judge the world, didn't come to us in that role at his first coming. His chief desire was to save us from the consequences of our wrong choices and our rejection of God. He paid our debts with his life, and now he's waiting for us to do our part—to turn around and be reconciled to God before the final judgment.

What man of you, having an hundred sheep, if he lose one of them, doth not leave the ninety and nine in the wilderness, and go after that which is lost, until he find it? And when he hath found it, he layeth it on his shoulders, rejoicing. And when he cometh home, he calleth together his friends and neighbours, saying unto them, Rejoice with me; for I have found my sheep which was lost.

—Luke 15:4-6

Lord, this is one of those days when I really don't know which way to turn. I've lost my sense of direction and I'm wondering which trail will take me back to familiar ground. Lead me, Lord. Send the signs I need to follow to get where you want me to go. I put my trust in you.

Ye have heard that it hath been said, An eye for an eye, and a tooth for a tooth: But I say unto you, That ye resist not evil: but whosoever shall smite thee on thy right cheek, turn to him the other also. And if any man will sue thee at the law, and take away thy coat, let him have thy cloak also. And whosoever shall compel thee to go a mile, go with him twain. Give to him that asketh thee, and from him that would borrow of thee turn not thou away.

—Matthew 5:38-42

Give me the tools for building peace. In your wisdom I daily try to impart, needed tools include a kind of heart and faith that measures each tiny rebuilt bridge a triumph.

I am the good shepherd: the good shepherd giveth his life for the sheep. But he that is an hireling, and not the shepherd, whose own the sheep are not, seeth the wolf coming, and leaveth the sheep, and fleeth: and the wolf catcheth them, and scattereth the sheep. The hireling fleeth, because he is an hireling, and careth not for the sheep.

—John 10:11-13

Despite today's valley of shadow and sickness, I know you, good shepherd of my soul, will continue restoring me as I move through treatment into the safe meadow of wellness.

Whosoever shall say unto this mountain, Be thou removed, and be thou cast into the sea; and shall not doubt in his heart, but shall believe that those things which he saith shall come to pass; he shall have whatsoever he saith.

—Mark 11:23

Father, you will help us to survive the seasons of surprises in our lives. For just as the harshest winter always gives way to the warm blush of spring, the season of our suffering will give way to a brighter tomorrow, where change becomes a catalyst for new growth and spiritual maturity. Amen.

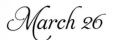

And when Jesus had cried with a loud
voice, he said, Father, into thy hands I commend
my spirit: and having said thus, he gave up
the ghost.

—Luke 23:46

You gave us the incredible gift of your son, Father
God. Thank you. What do I need to put in your hands?
What do I need to release to you? With what do I need
to trust you?

> Whosoever therefore shall confess me before men, him will I confess also before my Father which is in heaven. But whosoever shall deny me before men, him will I also deny before my Father which is in heaven.
>
> —Matthew 10:32-33

Dear Lord, may I always remember that self-realization is achieved through my service to you.

> **Yet a little while is the light with you. Walk while ye have the light, lest darkness come upon you: for he that walketh in darkness knoweth not whither he goeth.**
>
> **—John 12:35**

God, thank you for giving me this light of mine to shine. I promise never to conceal the brilliance you've bestowed upon me. May I forever reflect the glow of your loving presence. Amen.

> The Son of man is delivered into the hands of men, and they shall kill him; and after that he is killed, he shall rise the third day.
>
> —Mark 9:31

Jesus, you are at once awe-inspiring and a friend. Your words bring both challenging truth and peaceful comfort. I think of the innocent baby born in a manger, the man who died for us, and the miracle of your resurrection.

> **Whosoever exalteth himself shall be abased;
> and he that humbleth himself shall be exalted.**
>
> —Luke 14:11

Lord, I ask that you give me the gift of humility. Sometimes I get full of myself as if I have it all figured out. Lord, you are the one who grants me the grace to walk on this path. You are the one who draws me back when I stumble. My best efforts pale next to your grace.

There went out a sower to sow: And it came
to pass, as he sowed, some fell by the way side,
and the fowls of the air came and devoured it
up. And some fell on stony ground, where it had
not much earth; and immediately it sprang up,
because it had no depth of earth: But when the
sun was up, it was scorched; and because it had
no root, it withered away. And some fell among
thorns, and the thorns grew up, and choked it,
and it yielded no fruit. And other fell on good
ground, and did yield fruit that sprang up
and increased.

—Mark 4:3-8

Lord, draw me to your Word! Give me a thirst for
righteousness. I want to grow according to your ways,
seeking your path instead of following my own. I want
to choose to walk with you.

April

Are ye so without understanding also? Do ye not perceive, that whatsoever thing from without entereth into the man, it cannot defile him; Because it entereth not into his heart, but into the belly, and goeth out into the draught, purging all meats? And he said, That which cometh out of the man, that defileth the man. For from within, out of the heart of men, proceed evil thoughts, adulteries, fornications, murders, thefts, covetousness, wickedness, deceit, lasciviousness, an evil eye, blasphemy, pride, foolishness: All these evil things come from within, and defile the man.

—Mark 7:18-23

Seek the goodness that only God can put in your heart. When you operate from your own will, you grow tired and weary. When you accept God's will, you feel as though the floodgates have opened and you are floating downstream, relaxed and in the flow of blessings!

For a good tree bringeth not forth corrupt fruit; neither doth a corrupt tree bring forth good fruit. For every tree is known by his own fruit. For of thorns men do not gather figs, nor of a bramble bush gather they grapes. A good man out of the good treasure of his heart bringeth forth that which is good; and an evil man out of the evil treasure of his heart bringeth forth that which is evil: for of the abundance of the heart his mouth speaketh.

—Luke 6:43-45

Lord, please help me to remember that you are the source of all good things that come out of my life as I grow and flourish in you. All the "good fruit" of love, joy, peace, patience, kindness, goodness, faithfulness, gentleness, and self-control come directly from you. I want to thank your presence for nourishing and supporting my life.

> **Yet a little while am I with you, and then I go unto him that sent me. Ye shall seek me, and shall not find me: and where I am, thither ye cannot come.**
>
> —John 7:33-34

Lord, how we love to contemplate your sojourn on earth. How you were present in the lives of those who walked with you and attentive to the unspoken needs of every heart. How we love to tell of your sacrifice on the cross so that all of us might one day share eternal life with you. It's the story that has the power to save, the power to transform hearts.

**Blessed are the poor in spirit:
for theirs is the kingdom of heaven.**

—Matthew 5:3

I want to be independent, self-reliant, and competent.
I want to be talented. But without you, God, I have
nothing. Please never let me forget that any gift that
I have comes from you. Please help me let go of all
things that are not from you, and accept with humility
my dependence on you.

If a son shall ask bread of any of you that is a father, will he give him a stone? or if he ask a fish, will he for a fish give him a serpent? Or if he shall ask an egg, will he offer him a scorpion? If ye then, being evil, know how to give good gifts unto your children: how much more shall your heavenly Father give the Holy Spirit to them that ask him?

—Luke 11:11-13

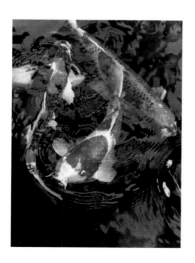

God, I come to you today giving thanks for all the blessings you've bestowed upon my family. Even through the challenges, your presence reminds us we can get through anything with you to lead us. I am forever grateful for the love and grace and mercy you've continued to show us.

> **Thou art not far from the kingdom of God.**
>
> **—Mark 12:34**

Wherever you go, wherever you look, wherever you travel, wherever you tread—whether to the left or to the right, whether up to the sky or down to the sea—God is already there, waiting for you to arrive.

Foxes have holes, and birds of the air
have nests; but the Son of man hath not
where to lay his head.

—Luke 9:58

I am so grateful for my home! It may not be fancy, but
it is my own place. How lucky I am to have a place to
live safely. How good it is sometimes to retreat from the
world and be alone with my things, my routines, and
my space. Thank you, Lord, for giving me shelter and a
place to call my own.

Except ye eat the flesh of the Son of man, and drink his blood, ye have no life in you. Whoso eateth my flesh, and drinketh my blood, hath eternal life; and I will raise him up at the last day. For my flesh is meat indeed, and my blood is drink indeed. He that eateth my flesh, and drinketh my blood, dwelleth in me, and I in him. As the living Father hath sent me, and I live by the Father: so he that eateth me, even he shall live by me. This is that bread which came down from heaven: not as your fathers did eat manna, and are dead: he that eateth of this bread shall live for ever.

—John 6:53-58

We praise you, Lord, for eternal life. We thank you for your love for each one of us. O God, it is reassuring to know that you sent your only son Jesus to guide, direct, and hear our voices.

> If the salt have lost his savour, wherewith shall it be salted? it is thenceforth good for nothing, but to be cast out, and to be trodden under foot of men.
>
> —Matthew 5:13

God, you warn in Revelation against the dangers of a lukewarm faith. Keep me from losing my savor. Let me always serve you with joy and attentiveness and fervor, paying attention to my prayers instead of saying them by rote.

> Now is the judgment of this world: now shall the prince of this world be cast out. And I, if I be lifted up from the earth, will draw all men unto me.
>
> —John 12:31-32

Jesus, every time I stop to think of it, I am awed that you provided salvation for us at the price of your own life. Thank you for opening up the way for me to enjoy eternal life with you. May my being be filled with joy, gratitude, and awe at every mention of your name.

Daughters of Jerusalem, weep not for me,
but weep for yourselves, and for your children.
For, behold, the days are coming, in the which
they shall say, Blessed are the barren, and the
wombs that never bare, and the paps which
never gave suck. Then shall they begin to say to
the mountains, Fall on us; and to the hills, Cover
us. For if they do these things in a green tree,
what shall be done in the dry?

—Luke 23:28-31

No one knows the mind of God, nor why he chooses to work the way he does. But in our most difficult circumstances, we will miss the peace of his presence unless we persevere in trusting that he is always faithful and always good.

> Behold, we go up to Jerusalem; and the Son of man shall be delivered unto the chief priests, and unto the scribes; and they shall condemn him to death, and shall deliver him to the Gentiles: And they shall mock him, and shall scourge him, and shall spit upon him, and shall kill him: and the third day he shall rise again.
>
> —Mark 10:33-34

Jesus had promised his followers that he would die, then rise again. On that morning—that mind-blowing morning—when Jesus exited his tomb in triumph over our nemesis death, there was no doubt that he had meant what he had said. "Look!" the angel exclaimed. In other words, "See for yourself that it's true." Jesus has risen, and he opened the way to eternal life for all who trust in him.

> **Verily, verily, I say unto thee, Except a man be born again, he cannot see the kingdom of God.**
>
> —John 3:3

I am feeling tired and weary and weak. I do my best each day, and often it just doesn't seem good enough. I lose hope and enthusiasm and a sense of purpose to carry on. I pray today for restored hope in my heart, and a new vision of possibility in my soul. I pray for a rejuvenated body with energy to continue to pursue my passions and dreams. Give me hope again, God, because my life is not over yet. Take my hand and pull me up just enough that I can get on my feet again and keep moving forward into the future.

> He that denieth me before men shall be denied before the angels of God. And whosoever shall speak a word against the Son of man, it shall be forgiven him: but unto him that blasphemeth against the Holy Ghost it shall not be forgiven.
>
> —Luke 12:9-10

Make me strong in body and in spirit. Give me a faith that never weakens, and a courage that never wavers. Help me, Lord, to be a rock to those who need me, as you always are to me. Help me to also help myself when no one is around, and to learn to lean on your wisdom and guidance rather than my own. Be my rock and my shield, guarding me from harm.

If thy right eye offend thee, pluck it out, and cast it from thee: for it is profitable for thee that one of thy members should perish, and not that thy whole body should be cast into hell. And if thy right hand offend thee, cut it off, and cast it from thee: for it is profitable for thee that one of thy members should perish, and not that thy whole body should be cast into hell.

—Matthew 5:29-30

Temptations are everywhere, God. Please stay nearby so that your power keeps me strong.

> **Render to Caesar the things that are Caesar's,**
> **and to God the things that are God's.**
>
> —Mark 12:17

My heart belongs to you, Lord. Do not let my many earthly possessions and concerns cloud my devotion to my faith.

Ye are from beneath; I am from above: ye
are of this world; I am not of this world. I said
therefore unto you, that ye shall die in your sins:
for if ye believe not that I am he, ye shall die in
your sins.

—John 8:23-24

God sent his son to Earth to deliver his message of love
personally. When he died for us, he was saying through
his action, "I love you." God remains always ready to
lavish his love on his children. May you open your
heart to receive all the love he has to offer.

> Agree with thine adversary quickly, whiles thou art in the way with him; lest at any time the adversary deliver thee to the judge, and the judge deliver thee to the officer, and thou be cast into prison. Verily I say unto thee, Thou shalt by no means come out thence, till thou hast paid the uttermost farthing.
>
> —Matthew 5:25-26

Growing in wisdom means growing in love, tolerance, grace, and acceptance.

> But when they shall lead you, and deliver you up, take no thought beforehand what ye shall speak, neither do ye premeditate: but whatsoever shall be given you in that hour, that speak ye: for it is not ye that speak, but the Holy Ghost.
>
> —Mark 13:11

Lord, help me remember that you are the God of hope. You don't want me to feel sad or hopeless. It isn't your plan for me to live in fear or doubt. Help me to feel and access the power of the Holy Spirit. I know that through your Spirit I will find the hope and joy and peace you have promised to your people.

He that entereth in by the door is the shepherd of the sheep. To him the porter openeth; and the sheep hear his voice: and he calleth his own sheep by name, and leadeth them out. And when he putteth forth his own sheep, he goeth before them, and the sheep follow him: for they know his voice. And a stranger will they not follow, but will flee from him: for they know not the voice of strangers.

—John 10:2-5

Thank you, Father, for your Holy Spirit, who guides me through each day. May I willingly follow his lead, no matter when or where. Help me to obey quickly when he directs me to serve or forgive others. May I always be thankful and rejoice in the blessings he points out to me along the way.

> Why are ye troubled? and why do thoughts
> arise in your hearts? Behold my hands and
> my feet, that it is I myself: handle me, and
> see; for a spirit hath not flesh and bones,
> as ye see me have.
>
> —Luke 24:38-39

God of my life, though you are not visible to me, I see evidence of your existence everywhere I look. You speak to me in silent ways with an inaudible voice. How can I explain this mystery—what I know to be true but cannot prove? This spiritual sensitivity—this awareness of you—is more real to me than the pages on which my eyes fall at this moment. You exist, and I believe.

Verily, verily, I say unto you, Ye seek me, not because ye saw the miracles, but because ye did eat of the loaves, and were filled. Labour not for the meat which perisheth, but for that meat which endureth unto everlasting life, which the Son of man shall give unto you: for him hath God the Father sealed.

—John 6:26-27

Lord, you know all things—from beginning to end—for you are the eternal, all-knowing God. I don't need to fear what is yet to come because I belong to you, and you have given me the gift of eternal life. I come to you today to be refreshed by your presence and your Word.

Except ye be converted, and become as little children, ye shall not enter into the kingdom of heaven. Whosoever therefore shall humble himself as this little child, the same is greatest in the kingdom of heaven. And whoso shall receive one such little child in my name receiveth me. But whoso shall offend one of these little ones which believe in me, it were better for him that a millstone were hanged about his neck, and that he were drowned in the depth of the sea.

—Matthew 18:3-6

Bless the children, God of little ones, with their giggles and wide-eyed awe, their awaking assumption that today will be chock-full of surprises, learning, and love. Neither missing nor wasting a minute, they take nothing for granted, a message that blesses us.

Marvel not that I said unto thee, Ye must be born again. The wind bloweth where it listeth, and thou hearest the sound thereof, but canst not tell whence it cometh, and whither it goeth: so is every one that is born of the Spirit.

—John 3:7-8

The mind is like a garden of fertile soil into which the seeds of our thoughts, ideas, and intentions are planted. With loving care and nurturing attention, those seeds bloom forth to manifest in our lives as wonderful opportunities and events. Those seeds that we choose to either ignore or neglect will simply die off. Thus, God turns over old growth into new, casting off new seeds to one day bloom forth in a cycle of renewal and abundance.

Whosoever shall receive one of
such children in my name, receiveth me:
and whosoever shall receive me,
receiveth not me, but him that sent me.

—Mark 9:37

Heavenly Father, just for today, please keep my eyes
open, my hands willing, and my heart eager to help
everyone in need who crosses my path, even if the need
is as small as an encouraging smile, even if the need
requires a sacrifice of time and talent. Just for today,
God. With your guidance, I have faith that, day by day,
I can help more and give more.

Blessed are ye, when men shall revile you, and persecute you, and shall say all manner of evil against you falsely, for my sake.

—Matthew 5:11

Where in my life am I nudged by others to ignore your Word, or look the other way? Please grant me the courage to stand up for your truth, regardless of consequence.

I am the true vine, and my Father is the husbandman. Every branch in me that beareth not fruit he taketh away: and every branch that beareth fruit, he purgeth it, that it may bring forth more fruit. Now ye are clean through the word which I have spoken unto you. Abide in me, and I in you. As the branch cannot bear fruit of itself, except it abide in the vine; no more can ye, except ye abide in me.

—John 15:1-4

What "speaks" to you in nature? The smell of the air after a rainstorm? The night sky? Maybe you simply wonder how those weeds can find a way to thrive in the cracks of the sidewalk. Whatever impresses us among the things God has made, it's a part of his messaging system to us, inviting us to search him out and find relationship with him.

> If any man desire to be first, the same shall be last of all, and servant of all.
>
> —Mark 9:35

It is hard to be patient, but I am grateful for that gift. Whether it is waiting in line or anticipating a coming event, patience is a wonderful way to slow down and appreciate what is coming. Thank you for the gift of patience and the ability to take my time and savor every moment. Instead of saying, "I can't wait!" I am happy to say, "I will wait my turn" as I anticipate what is to come.

Destroy this temple, and in three days
I will raise it up.

—John 2:19

Heavenly Father, your son, Jesus, could have called down heaven to destroy his enemies when he was on earth, but he didn't. Revenge wasn't his mission. Love was. Help me to submit, as he did, to a path of gentleness in the strength of your love. Amen.

> **Thomas, because thou hast seen me, thou hast believed: blessed are they that have not seen, and yet have believed.**
>
> **—John 20:29**

Faith is knowing without seeing, believing without fully understanding, trusting without touching the one who is ever faithful.

May

O righteous Father, the world hath not known thee: but I have known thee, and these have known that thou hast sent me. And I have declared unto them thy name, and will declare it: that the love wherewith thou hast loved me may be in them, and I in them.

—John 17:25-26

Through the eyes of faith we see the company we keep.

> The Son of man is as a man taking a far journey, who left his house, and gave authority to his servants, and to every man his work, and commanded the porter to watch. Watch ye therefore: for ye know not when the master of the house cometh, at even, or at midnight, or at the cockcrowing, or in the morning: Lest coming suddenly he find you sleeping. And what I say unto you I say unto all, Watch.
>
> —Mark 13:34-37

Jesus, your purposes are eternal ones, and they're generally the opposite of an earthbound here-and-now mind-set. It takes a committed heart and soul to

follow you. So where I have become dusty or rusty in my attentiveness in following you, please come with the breath of your Spirit to refresh me and get me moving in your ways again.

Go your ways: behold, I send you forth as lambs among wolves. Carry neither purse, nor scrip, nor shoes: and salute no man by the way. And into whatsoever house ye enter, first say, Peace be to this house. And if the son of peace be there, your peace shall rest upon it: if not, it shall turn to you again. And in the same house remain, eating and drinking such things as they give: for the labourer is worthy of his hire.

—Luke 10:3-7

Father, thank you for initiating our wonderful relationship by loving me first! Your perfect love has taught me to trust you and leave my fear of your judgment behind. Your love for me brings such joy to my life, Lord. Help me spread this joy to others today.

My doctrine is not mine, but his that sent me. If any man will do his will, he shall know of the doctrine, whether it be of God, or whether I speak of myself. He that speaketh of himself seeketh his own glory: but he that seeketh his glory that sent him, the same is true, and no unrighteousness is in him.

—John 7:16-18

Father, your Word makes it clear to me that the life of faith is not passive. While we wait for you to answer prayer, grant wisdom, and open doors, we also keep our minds sharp and our hearts strengthened by reading and studying your Word, by meeting with you in prayer, and by finding encouragement among other believers. These are the disciplines our souls need to stay focused on ever-present hope.

> **Blessed are the pure in heart:**
> **for they shall see God.**
>
> —**Matthew 5:8**

When I read this beatitude, I think of my grandmother and her warm, radiant smile. Though she was a busy woman with a number of hobbies, she spent time in prayer every morning and every evening, and that prayer time was her spiritual anchor. More than that, when she saw something beautiful, she spontaneously

praised God. When something good happened, words of gratitude sprang from her lips. What a beautiful example she was, of someone in tune with God's will.

> **For whosoever shall do the will of God, the same is my brother, and my sister, and mother.**
>
> —Mark 3:35

Father, unity among your people is precious to you—and precious to us as well. We cannot achieve it without your assistance, though. Help us to keep petty disagreements from dividing us. Give us the grace to work through any disagreement with love and understanding.

Art thou the Christ? tell us. And he said unto them, If I tell you, ye will not believe: And if I also ask you, ye will not answer me, nor let me go. Hereafter shall the Son of man sit on the right hand of the power of God.

—Luke 22:67-69

How joyful life becomes when we surrender to our faith in God, allowing his will to work through us. We give up resistance and frustration, and things suddenly seem to flow with greater ease. We still have obstacles, but also the strength and resources to overcome them. Living in faith and experiencing more peace and joy is what God intended for us!

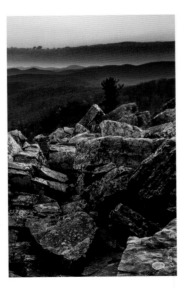

I can of mine own self do nothing: as I hear, I judge: and my judgment is just; because I seek not mine own will, but the will of the Father which hath sent me. If I bear witness of myself, my witness is not true. There is another that beareth witness of me; and I know that the witness which he witnesseth of me is true.

—John 5:30-32

All things are possible to those who have faith. Putting our trust in God gives us wings to soar higher, dream bigger, and go farther than we thought we ever could.

We rest in faith, knowing that whatever we need will be given to us in God's due time. What a wonderful feeling, to have an unshakeable faith and an immovable trust in his will for us!

As many as I love, I rebuke and chasten: be zealous therefore, and repent.

—**Revelation 3:19**

Here we are again, Lord. Another time when I feel like I've made a complete mess of this life you've given me. I place myself in your hands. If you need to totally reshape me to turn me into someone more useful, so be it! Thank you for not abandoning me, your humble creation. Make me over in your design.

He that rejecteth me, and receiveth not my words, hath one that judgeth him: the word that I have spoken, the same shall judge him in the last day. For I have not spoken of myself; but the Father which sent me, he gave me a commandment, what I should say, and what I should speak. And I know that his commandment is life everlasting: whatsoever I speak therefore, even as the Father said unto me, so I speak.

—John 12:48-50

I pray for the courage to stand against injustices and to reach out to my fellow humans without fear or concern of the repercussions.

> Blessed are they which are persecuted for righteousness' sake: for theirs is the kingdom of heaven.
>
> —**Matthew 5:10**

Lord, I get frustrated sometimes, when others are not acting rightly. But you never promised an easy road for those who believe in you. Let me be gentle but persistent in carrying your truth to the world, and not wither in the face of scorn.

When the unclean spirit is gone out of a man, he walketh through dry places, seeking rest; and finding none, he saith, I will return unto my house whence I came out. And when he cometh, he findeth it swept and garnished. Then goeth he, and taketh to him seven other spirits more wicked than himself; and they enter in, and dwell there: and the last state of that man is worse than the first.

—Luke 11:24-26

Lord, so often we find ourselves asking you to save us from bad situations only to discover you quietly revealing to us that we are our own worst enemies! Teach us to break destructive habits and to stop polluting our minds with negative thoughts, Lord. Save us from our enemies, even when it means you have to step in and save us from ourselves!

> I am the door: by me if any man enter in, he shall be saved, and shall go in and out, and find pasture. The thief cometh not, but for to steal, and to kill, and to destroy: I am come that they might have life, and that they might have it more abundantly.
>
> —John 10:9-10

An open door is an invitation. Just as the gates of heaven are open to all who follow God's will, an open door invites me in to experience new joys and revelations. Thank you, God, for allowing me to see the open doors in my life and take advantage of new experiences. Let me walk through them with Jesus at my side.

So is the kingdom of God, as if a man should cast seed into the ground; And should sleep, and rise night and day, and the seed should spring and grow up, he knoweth not how. For the earth bringeth forth fruit of herself; first the blade, then the ear, after that the full corn in the ear. But when the fruit is brought forth, immediately he putteth in the sickle, because the harvest is come.

—Mark 4:26-29

When surrounded by nature's bounty, the heart discovers serenity, the soul knows abiding peace, and the spirit finds renewal.

> They that be whole need not a physician, but they that are sick. But go ye and learn what that meaneth, I will have mercy, and not sacrifice: for I am not come to call the righteous, but sinners to repentance.
>
> —Matthew 9:12-13

Help me, God, to see that you gave your love in such a way that even the most wicked person can repent and find new life in your grace and mercy; indeed, that your love calls even the worst sinners to become your children. You created each person with a specific purpose to serve in this world. Help me, Lord, to pray that each person will turn away from evil, turn to you, and become your devoted servant. Amen.

Sanctify them through thy truth: thy word is truth. As thou hast sent me into the world, even so have I also sent them into the world. And for their sakes I sanctify myself, that they also might be sanctified through the truth.

—John 17:17-19

Pursue truth, and you will find God.

But in those days, after that tribulation, the sun shall be darkened, and the moon shall not give her light, And the stars of heaven shall fall, and the powers that are in heaven shall be shaken. And then shall they see the Son of man coming in the clouds with great power and glory. And then shall he send his angels, and shall gather together his elect from the four winds, from the uttermost part of the earth to the uttermost part of heaven.

—Mark 13:24-27

Spiritual darkness is the deepest kind of darkness. One may live in the darkness of being physically blind and yet have the light of Christ, which brings meaning, joy, and hope. Without the light of Christ in a life, there is something missing in the soul.

He said unto the man, Stretch forth thy hand.
And he did so: and his hand was restored whole
as the other.

—Luke 6:10

Lord, I ask for your restoration today. Heal my body,
my mind, and my soul from injuries and old wounds. I
hold out my hands to you today.

The time cometh, when I shall no more speak unto you in proverbs, but I shall shew you plainly of the Father. At that day ye shall ask in my name: and I say not unto you, that I will pray the Father for you: For the Father himself loveth you, because ye have loved me, and have believed that I came out from God.

—John 16:25-27

God gives us faith as a means of getting in touch with his love. For once we have that love, we can pass it on to others.

> But to sit on my right hand and on my left hand is not mine to give; but it shall be given to them for whom it is prepared.
>
> —Mark 10:40

At the dawn of creation, God laid out his plans for the universe, and the plan is still working.

> Therefore also said the wisdom of God, I will send them prophets and apostles, and some of them they shall slay and persecute: That the blood of all the prophets, which was shed from the foundation of the world, may be required of this generation.
>
> —Luke 11:49-50

Sacrifice doesn't always come easily, Lord. Please show me those opportunities you have placed in my day for me to lay down my own to-do list and be aware of the greater things you are doing through me. Don't let me miss those opportunities, Lord. Please do not allow any grumbling on my part to deter your work. Grant me the grace to make any sacrifices you need from me today.

For the Father loveth the Son, and sheweth him all things that himself doeth: and he will shew him greater works than these, that ye may marvel. For as the Father raiseth up the dead, and quickeneth them; even so the Son quickeneth whom he will. For the Father judgeth no man, but hath committed all judgment unto the Son: That all men should honour the Son, even as they honour the Father. He that honoureth not the Son honoureth not the Father which hath sent him.

—John 5:20-23

Father God, you gave a staggering gift through your son, Jesus Christ. How can I express my gratitude for the gift of salvation? Sometimes I need to sit in silence, surrounded by your presence, as I reflect on your love for me.

> **Blessed are the merciful:**
> **for they shall obtain mercy.**
>
> —**Matthew 5:7**

For those times when friends or family members have forgiven me when I wronged them, I offer thanks and ask your blessings upon them. They taught me about how powerful mercy can be. O merciful God, let me in turn be merciful to others.

> As long as I am in the world,
> I am the light of the world.
>
> —**John 9:5**

No darkness is black enough to hide you, Lord, for there is always light even if I sometimes misplace it. Just when I'm ready to give up, there it shines through caregivers, family, friends; through my renewed energy to choose treatments and recovery. I'm absolutely certain you are the sender of this light.

> When ye see a cloud rise out of the west, straightway ye say, There cometh a shower; and so it is. And when ye see the south wind blow, ye say, There will be heat; and it cometh to pass. Ye hypocrites, ye can discern the face of the sky and of the earth; but how is it that ye do not discern this time?
>
> —Luke 12:54-56

Lord, it often happens that you are trying to communicate an important truth to us, but we are so busy searching for the truth elsewhere that we don't stop and listen. Teach us the importance of being still, Lord. Only when we are still can we be aware of your presence and hear your voice. Speak to us, Lord—and help us be ready to listen.

For I say unto you, That except your righteousness shall exceed the righteousness of the scribes and Pharisees, ye shall in no case enter into the kingdom of heaven.

—Matthew 5:20

True faith is demonstrated when we look for ways to be kind to those in need.

> When ye have lifted up the Son of man, then shall ye know that I am he, and that I do nothing of myself; but as my Father hath taught me, I speak these things. And he that sent me is with me: the Father hath not left me alone; for I do always those things that please him.
>
> —John 8:28-29

Son of God, who came to Earth,
thank you for your love for us.

Son of Man, who dwelt among us,
thank you for your love for us.

Savior, who redeemed the world,
thank you for your love for us.

Jesus, living Word of God,
thank you for your love for us.

A certain man had a fig tree planted in his vineyard; and he came and sought fruit thereon, and found none. Then said he unto the dresser of his vineyard, Behold, these three years I come seeking fruit on this fig tree, and find none: cut it down; why cumbereth it the ground? And he answering said unto him, Lord, let it alone this year also, till I shall dig about it, and dung it: And if it bear fruit, well: and if not, then after that thou shalt cut it down.

—Luke 13:6-9

God of second chances, even if my latest setback is a failure, with you, failure is never final but an opportunity

to learn and grow. When I goof, as I am prone to do, help me from doubling the problem by failing to take advantage of your redemption.

> **He that hath ears to hear, let him hear.**
>
> —**Mark 4:9**

Touch and calm my turbulent emotions, God of still waters. Whisper your words of guidance to the listening ears of my soul. In hearing your voice, give me assurance beyond a shadow of a doubt that you are my companion in life, eternally.

Strive to enter in at the strait gate:
for many, I say unto you, will seek to enter in,
and shall not be able.

—Luke 13:24

Pray that you will be God's instrument for bringing
good to your world.

> Enter ye in at the strait gate: for wide is
> the gate, and broad is the way, that leadeth to
> destruction, and many there be which go in
> thereat: Because strait is the gate, and narrow is
> the way, which leadeth unto life, and few there
> be that find it.
>
> —Matthew 7:13-14

Every day I'm exposed to a world whose values don't jibe with yours, Lord. I am in need of constant reminders to not get caught up in notions that money, power, status, and physical appearance are of utmost importance. Faithfulness to you is where real life is

lived out and lasting inner peace is achieved. O Lord, help me when I'm tempted to believe that I can prevail in life by being seen as "strong" in ways that ultimately don't matter to you.

June

I tell you, this man went down to his house justified rather than the other: for every one that exalteth himself shall be abased; and he that humbleth himself shall be exalted.

—Luke 18:14

Dear God, may I live a life of faith, cheer, and humility; help me to live in a way that uplifts others.

This is my commandment, That ye love one another, as I have loved you. Greater love hath no man than this, that a man lay down his life for his friends. Ye are my friends, if ye do whatsoever I <u>command</u> you. Henceforth I call you not servants; for the servant knoweth not what his lord doeth: but I have called you friends; for all things that I have heard of my Father I have made known unto you.

—John 15:12-15

You, O Lord, are a faithful, to-the-finish, forever friend.

> For whosoever will save his life shall lose it:
> but whosoever will lose his life for my sake, the
> same shall save it. For what is a man advantaged,
> if he gain the whole world, and lose himself, or
> be cast away?
>
> —Luke 9:24-25

One sentiment I hear from time to time is "...after all, we're all God's children." It's usually uttered during trying times, to remind us to hold on and keep the faith. It's a comforting thought, but the verse here stresses that God's children are led by his Spirit. May we strive each day to be active children of God, praying and following the call of his Spirit rather than our own impulses and desires.

> For whosoever shall be ashamed of me and of my words, of him shall the Son of man be ashamed, when he shall come in his own glory, and in his Father's, and of the holy angels. But I tell you of a truth, there be some standing here, which shall not taste of death, till they see the kingdom of God.
>
> —Luke 9:26-27

I align my plans with God's will for my life. I listen to his guidance and follow his lead. I take the steps he directs me to take, and face the lessons he asks me to learn. I evolve. I grow. I become!

> **And he saith unto them, <u>Follow me</u>, and I will make you fishers of men. And they straightway left their nets, and followed him.**
>
> **—Matthew 4:19–20**

Jesus, when you call me, let me respond, like Peter and Andrew, immediately! I get so immersed in life's minutiae sometimes. I put off prayer or spending time with you, because I tell myself that I have just one more thing that I need to do first. When I feel the impulse to pray, let me stop where I am and pray. Let me never forget that, before anything else, I am called to be your follower.

> **Have faith in God.**
>
> —Mark 11:22

When a task requiring faith confronts us, <u>voices</u> around us may say, "It can't be done." The voices may even come from within us, and we may want to quit before we start. But if we hold on to faith, we can succeed, no matter what the critics say.

Satan

Verily, verily, I say unto thee, We speak that we do know, and testify that we have seen; and ye receive not our witness. If I have told you earthly things, and ye believe not, how shall ye believe, if I tell you of heavenly things? And no man hath ascended up to heaven, but he that came down from heaven, even the Son of man which is in heaven. And as Moses lifted up the serpent in the wilderness, even so must the Son of man be lifted up: That whosoever believeth in him should not perish, but have eternal life.

—John 3:11-15

Thank you, Lord, for making the things of heaven available to those who seek them.

> And he sighed deeply in his spirit, and saith,
> Why doth this generation seek after a sign?
> verily I say unto you, There shall no sign be
> given unto this generation.
>
> —Mark 8:12

Lord, how I long to stand strong in the faith! I read of the martyrs of old and question my own loyalty and courage. Would I, if my life hung in the balance, say, "Yes, I believe in God"? I pray I would, Lord. Continue to prepare me for any opportunity to stand firm for what I know to be true. To live without conviction is hardly to live at all.

I will give unto him that is athirst of the
fountain of the water of life freely.

—**Revelation 21:6**

In my hour of need, I turn my eyes inward to a place
where God's strength flows like a river of healing
waters. I immerse myself in the current, and at once I
am renewed.

> Whosoever drinketh of this water shall thirst again: But whosoever drinketh of the water that I shall give him shall never thirst; but the water that I shall give him shall be in him a well of water springing up into everlasting life.
>
> —John 4:13-14

Jesus' peace is here for me. He gave it to those who follow him as an assurance of his abiding presence. Will I choose to give it its place in my soul when troublesome things are jumping out at me or nipping at my heels? God, you have provided a great ocean of peace for my soul.

He that believeth and is baptized shall be saved; but he that believeth not shall be damned. And these signs shall follow them that believe; In my name shall they cast out devils; they shall speak with new tongues; They shall take up serpents; and if they drink any deadly thing, it shall not hurt them; they shall lay hands on the sick, and they shall recover.

—Mark 16:16-18

Lord, the world just wasn't ready for your appearance by the Jordan. There you were, the king they so desired, yet they didn't know you. Let us welcome you as wholeheartedly as John the Baptist did! For you came to be our hope and our salvation. Humbly he came, but mightily he saved.

> He said unto them, Ye will surely
> say unto me this proverb, Physician, heal thyself:
> whatsoever we have heard done in Capernaum,
> do also here in thy country. And he said,
> Verily I say unto you, No prophet is accepted in
> his own country.
>
> —Luke 4:23-24

Jesus, I believe you can help me. I trust that you will provide resources for my healing. I am ready to do what I need to do to be healed. Amen.

The works that I do in my Father's name, they bear witness of me. But ye believe not, because ye are not of my sheep, as I said unto you. My sheep hear my voice, and I know them, and they follow me: And I give unto them eternal life; and they shall never perish, neither shall any man pluck them out of my hand. My Father, which gave them me, is greater than all; and no man is able to pluck them out of my Father's hand. I and my Father are one.

—John 10:25-30

Each life that touches ours for good is a reflection of God's love for us.

Whosoever will come after me, let him deny himself, and take up his cross, and follow me. For whosoever will save his life shall lose it; but whosoever shall lose his life for my sake and the gospel's, the same shall save it. For what shall it profit a man, if he shall gain the whole world, and lose his own soul? Or what shall a man give in exchange for his soul? Whosoever therefore shall be ashamed of me and of my words in this adulterous and sinful generation; of him also shall the Son of man be ashamed, when he cometh in the glory of his Father with the holy angels.

—Mark 8:34-38

God teaches us that love is a two-way exchange of something profound: its very nature is selfless and humble. Love isn't the flash and show; it's a grounded exchange, a deep, mutual caring and respect that endures long after the first brilliant connection.

And he said unto Jesus, Lord, remember me when thou comest into thy kingdom. And Jesus said unto him, Verily I say unto thee, Today shalt thou be with me in paradise.

—Luke 23:42–43

In extremity, one of the men crucified next to Jesus admitted his wrongdoings and made a connection with Jesus. When I feel like I am too far gone in sin to turn back, and I shouldn't bother with repentance, let me remember this example. It's never too late to seek out Jesus for love, guidance, and forgiveness.

**Blessed are the meek:
for they shall inherit the earth.**

—Matthew 5:5

Please grant me a listening spirit. With my spouse,
my children, my friends, let me be someone they can
approach with problems and questions, knowing I will
be gentle with them. Let me be appreciative when I
hear others express wisdom and insight, rather than
always having to be the person to have the answers
myself. And when I am called to lead, let me lead with
love and a listening ear to the concerns of others.

> **Moses gave you not that bread from heaven; but my Father giveth you the true bread from heaven. For the bread of God is he which cometh down from heaven, and giveth life unto the world.**
>
> **—John 6:32-33**

God of providence, I may appease my family's physical hunger, but only you satisfy their hungry hearts with heavenly food—"the Bread of Life"—your son, Jesus Christ. Amen.

Whosoever cometh to me, and heareth my sayings, and doeth them, I will shew you to whom he is like: He is like a man which built an house, and digged deep, and laid the foundation on a rock: and when the flood arose, the stream beat vehemently upon that house, and could not shake it: for it was founded upon a rock. But he that heareth, and doeth not, is like a man that without a foundation built an house upon the earth; against which the stream did beat vehemently, and immediately it fell; and the ruin of that house was great.

—Luke 6:47-49

God recognizes and rewards faithful work.

> I go my way, and ye shall seek me, and shall
> die in your sins: whither I go, ye cannot come.
>
> —John 8:21

No one likes suffering. But it brings our attention back to God and reminds us how helpless we are without his presence and love.

Take heed that ye despise not one of these little ones; for I say unto you, That in heaven their angels do always behold the face of my Father which is in heaven. For the Son of man is come to save that which was lost.

—Matthew 18:10-11

We should always thank the Lord for the faith of others.

Now learn a parable of the fig tree; When her branch is yet tender, and putteth forth leaves, ye know that summer is near: So ye in like manner, when ye shall see these things come to pass, know that it is nigh, even at the doors.

—Mark 13:28-29

Thank you for the bright colors of summer! I look around and see the sun in the sky, the clear moon in the night, the brilliance of the flowers and the trees. Thank you, Lord, for blessing me with color in my life. I know that even the darkest, dreariest days cannot last forever, just as the memory of winter fades during summer's glory.

> **He that heareth my word, and believeth on him that sent me, hath everlasting life, and shall not come into condemnation; but is passed from death unto life.**
>
> —John 5:24

When the night is dark and cold, and the days promise little rest, be strong, because God has made you a promise of a mighty kingdom on the other side. Work hard, keep moving, and never let others derail you from your mission.

> Who then is that faithful and wise steward, whom his lord shall make ruler over his household, to give them their portion of meat in due season? Blessed is that servant, whom his lord when he cometh shall find so doing. Of a truth I say unto you, that he will make him ruler over all that he hath.
>
> —Luke 12:42-44

Faith is a key that opens the door of abundance. Too many of us live behind locked doors of lack, suffering, and loneliness when everything we could possibly desire is on the other side. God has promised us abundant blessings, but first we must show him we have faith by moving towards the door without doubt, fear, and uncertainty. Then, he will reveal a bounty of blessings to reward us.

Let not your heart be troubled: ye believe in God, believe also in me. In my Father's house are many mansions: if it were not so, I would have told you. I go to prepare a place for you. And if I go and prepare a place for you, I will come again, and receive you unto myself; that where I am, there ye may be also. And whither I go ye know, and the way ye know.

—John 14:1-4

Sing the wondrous love of Jesus,
Sing his mercy and his grace;
In the mansions bright and blessed,
He'll prepare for us a place.
—Eliza E. Hewitt, "When We All Get To Heaven"

June 25

> Judge not, that ye be not judged. For with what judgment ye judge, ye shall be judged: and with what measure ye mete, it shall be measured to you again. And why beholdest thou the mote that is in thy brother's eye, but considerest not the beam that is in thine own eye? Or how wilt thou say to thy brother, Let me pull out the mote out of thine eye; and, behold, a beam is in thine own eye? Thou hypocrite, first cast out the beam out of thine own eye; and then shalt thou see clearly to cast out the mote out of thy brother's eye.
>
> —Matthew 7:1-5

Give me a humble heart, Lord, so that I will not judge others—but please give me the gift of moral clarity as well, to seek to live by your values and do your will.

> **If ye do not forgive, neither will your Father which is in heaven forgive your trespasses.**
>
> —Mark 11:26

This directive is so hard, Lord. I want to live as you ask, but sometimes I long to see those who've hurt me "get what's coming to them." I desperately need you to help me refocus. When I am mired in bitterness, Lord, prod me to meditate on the mercy you've freely given me— even when I have been most undeserving. Then, Father, grant me the grace to love those who have done me harm—not because they deserve it, but because they are precious to you.

I am the vine, ye are the branches: He that abideth in me, and I in him, the same bringeth forth much fruit: for without me ye can do nothing. If a man abide not in me, he is cast forth as a branch, and is withered; and men gather them, and cast them into the fire, and they are burned. If ye abide in me, and my words abide in you, ye shall ask what ye will, and it shall be done unto you.

—John 15:5-7

Lord, I deeply desire to abide in you. I desire to have you abiding in me as well, so closely that I can speak to you any time and feel your presence. Destroy the distractions that create distance between us, Lord. Clear out the clutter that keeps me from sensing your best plan for my life.

> **Joy shall be in heaven over one sinner that repenteth, more than over ninety and nine just persons, which need no repentance.**
>
> **—Luke 15:7**

I am grateful that you don't require spiritual gymnastics from me when I sin, Lord. You just call me to come to you with a humble and repentant heart. In my pride I sometimes want to do something that will impress you—something that will "make up for it" somehow. But you just shake your head and keep calling me to humble myself and bring my sincere sorrow to you. That often doesn't seem like enough to me. But I guess that's the point: I can never earn your grace; it is a gift.

Well hath Esaias prophesied of you hypocrites, as it is written, This people honoureth me with their lips, but their heart is far from me. Howbeit in vain do they worship me, teaching for doctrines the commandments of men. For laying aside the commandment of God, ye hold the tradition of men, as the washing of pots and cups: and many other such like things ye do.

—Mark 7:6-8

When we shift our focus beyond the physical, we realize we exist amidst a presence and power that is transcendent.

> **Murmur not among yourselves. No man can come to me, except the Father which hath sent me draw him: and I will raise him up at the last day.**
>
> —John 6:43-44

The passing of a dear one often leaves us wondering "Why, God, why?" If we knew that death is the beginning of a new mystery, a new adventure to unfold, we would feel joy for those who leave this earth and joy for those yet to leave.

There is no man that hath left house, or brethren, or sisters, or father, or mother, or wife, or children, or lands, for my sake, and the gospel's, but he shall receive an hundredfold now in this time, houses, and brethren, and sisters, and mothers, and children, and lands, with persecutions; and in the world to come eternal life. But many that are first shall be last; and the last first.

—Mark 10:29-31

Lord, I've stood by too many deathbeds to doubt the adage "you can't take it with you." We come into this world with nothing, and we leave with nothing. So why is it so tempting to spend our lifetimes striving for more money and possessions? We forget that all those things are fleeting, and that the only people impressed by what we accumulate are those whose values are worldly. You, O God, are eternal!

All that the Father giveth me shall come to me; and him that cometh to me I will in no wise cast out. For I came down from heaven, not to do mine own will, but the will of him that sent me. And this is the Father's will which hath sent me, that of all which he hath given me I should lose nothing, but should raise it up again at the last day. And this is the will of him that sent me, that every one which seeth the Son, and believeth on him, may have everlasting life: and I will raise him up at the last day.

—John 6:37-40

Our delight in God's love cannot compare with his joy in loving us.

> **No man, having put his hand to the plough,
> and looking back, is fit for the kingdom of God.**
>
> —Luke 9:62

Have you ever met someone who solely defines themselves by their possessions? Though society may seem to reward those who achieve their self worth from having the "right" car, or the biggest house, these individuals are, at the root of it, unhappy people. Material gain in and of itself is, ultimately, an empty victory. Don't be that person. Don't let your worldly interests cloud your true sense of self.

> **Whosoever will be great among you, shall be your minister: And whosoever of you will be the chiefest, shall be servant of all.**
>
> **—Mark 10:43-44**

How blessed I am to live in the United States! Life may not always be easy, but I am grateful for the freedoms this nation gives to me. Thank you, Lord, for all the people who fought to make this country a free and beautiful land. I remember those patriots today as I listen to fireworks and enjoy my freedom. May I never take that freedom for granted.

> Give not that which is holy unto the dogs, neither cast ye your pearls before swine, lest they trample them under their feet, and turn again and rend you.
>
> —Matthew 7:6

Lord, I'm looking forward to sharing a home with you in the kingdom of heaven. Thank you for becoming poor so that I could become rich. Amen.

> **Behold, I come quickly; and my reward is with me, to give every man according as his work shall be.**
>
> **—Revelation 22:12**

God, the knowledge that your promises will be fulfilled keeps me going through the toughest of days and nights. I know if I stay strong and power through, I will be richly rewarded in body, mind, and spirit.

When ye pray, say, Our Father which art in heaven, Hallowed be thy name. Thy kingdom come. Thy will be done, as in heaven, so in earth. Give us day by day our daily bread. And forgive us our sins; for we also forgive every one that is indebted to us. And lead us not into temptation; but deliver us from evil.

—Luke 11:2-4

How good it is to talk to God! Formal prayer is important, but today I just want to pour out my heart and speak to God in my own words. Thank you for the

opportunity to talk to you as a friend. Thank you for listening to my prayers and understanding my heart.

I pray for them: I pray not for the world, but for them which thou hast given me; for they are thine. And all mine are thine, and thine are mine; and I am glorified in them. And now I am no more in the world, but these are in the world, and I come to thee.

—John 17:9-11

God, I ask in prayer that you help me hold the vision of a better world, and that I may clearly know my role in making that better world a reality. Let my vision join that of others, to create a more joyful world for those who come after us. Amen.

He cometh, and findeth them sleeping, and saith unto Peter, Simon, sleepest thou? couldest not thou watch one hour? Watch ye and pray, lest ye enter into temptation. The spirit truly is ready, but the flesh is weak.

—Mark 14:37-38

God, I hold fast to you at this present moment, for it is the only way for me to have perspective and hope for life beyond this pain I have. And yet, come quickly for I am tired. Fill me with your strength for I feel weak. Add meaning to these days of pain, and finally call me to a new day when I can serve you with a renewed purpose and passion. Amen.

> **He that believeth on me, believeth not on me, but on him that sent me. And he that seeth me seeth him that sent me.**
>
> **—John 12:44-45**

Lord, I seek the wisdom of understanding, and the grace of peace. The world is becoming a hostile place and only those armed with your loving care seem able to find their way. I ask from you a strong center from which I may go forth into the world and spread that same peace and that same understanding to others that need it so badly. Make me an instrument of your peace today, dear Lord. Let me help others find their center within where you reside, always loving, always caring, and forever present. Amen.

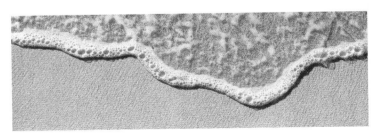

Jesus answered and said unto her, Martha,
Martha, thou art careful and troubled about
many things: But one thing is needful: and Mary
hath chosen that good part, which shall not be
taken away from her.

—Luke 10:41-42

I have Martha days and I have Mary days, Lord. Some
days lend themselves more to a worshipful response to
you than others do. But Mary didn't let everyday tasks
distract her from a golden opportunity to glean wisdom

from you, Lord.
Help me in
my quest to
carve out time
every day to be
attentive to your
Spirit. My to-do
list will always
be there on the
back burner.

Lay not up for yourselves treasures upon earth, where moth and rust doth corrupt, and where thieves break through and steal: But lay up for yourselves treasures in heaven, where neither moth nor rust doth corrupt, and where thieves do not break through nor steal: For where your treasure is, there will your heart be also.

—Matthew 6:19-21

I asked for God's greatest riches, and he gave me contentment.

The light of the body is the eye: if therefore thine eye be single, thy whole body shall be full of light. But if thine eye be evil, thy whole body shall be full of darkness. If therefore the light that is in thee be darkness, how great is that darkness! No man can serve two masters: for either he will hate the one, and love the other; or else he will hold to the one, and despise the other. Ye cannot serve God and mammon.

—Matthew 6:22-24

Creator God, you give me power to walk through dark valleys into the light. You give me hope when there seems no end to my suffering. You give me peace when my life overwhelms me. I ask that you give this same power, hope, and peace to all who know discouragement, that they, too, may be emboldened and renewed by your everlasting love.

July 14

> Why callest thou me good? there is none good
> but one, that is, God.
>
> —Mark 10:18

To be anointed in God's love is to be made into a powerful force for good. Be strong and go forward spreading light and love, for the world needs both now more than ever!

Ye call me Master and Lord: and ye say well;
for so I am. If I then, your Lord and Master,
have washed your feet; ye also ought to wash one
another's feet. For I have given you an example,
that ye should do as I have done to you.

—John 13:13-15

Love for God is the best motive for serving.

> **Whosoever doth not bear his cross, and come after me, cannot be my disciple.**
>
> —**Luke 14:27**

Lord, today I want to praise you for giving me the faith to believe, for faith itself is a gift from you. I lift up to you today all those I know who are having trouble accepting your gift of salvation. Be patient with them, Lord. Reveal yourself to them in a way that will reach them and draw them into a relationship with you. Our lives are incomplete without you, Lord. Send your grace to those who are struggling.

I am come in my Father's name, and ye receive me not: if another shall come in his own name, him ye will receive. How can ye believe, which receive honour one of another, and seek not the honour that cometh from God only?

—John 5:43-44

We thank and honor you, Lord, for your everlasting love and for the great sacrifice of your son, Jesus Christ. May we not stray from your guiding light.

> **Blessed is he that keepeth the sayings of the prophecy of this book.**
>
> —Revelation 22:7

God, you gave up your own beloved son for me. How could I possibly love with such a sense of sacrifice? Help me be the kind of person who can put the needs of others before my own. Help me give until it hurts. You have sacrificed for me—now let me give of myself in return. I know that in the end, I will be rewarded with your merciful grace. Amen.

> **The kingdom of heaven is like unto leaven,**
> **which a woman took, and hid in three measures**
> **of meal, till the whole was leavened.**
>
> **—Matthew 13:33**

All our lives we walk among heavenly beings, whether we believe in heaven or not. All our lives we are surrounded by individuals who spend their lives invisibly cheering us on.

This is the condemnation, that light is come into the world, and men loved darkness rather than light, because their deeds were evil. For every one that doeth evil hateth the light, neither cometh to the light, lest his deeds should be reproved. But he that doeth truth cometh to the light, that his deeds may be made manifest, that they are wrought in God.

—John 3:19-21

Thank you, Lord, for the inner light that shines within me. Help me to show that light to others and not hide it deep inside myself. Thank you for my talents and the things that I am good at. May I never forget how grateful I am to be able to share my abilities and bring joy to others.

If thy hand offend thee, cut it off: it is better for thee to enter into life maimed, than having two hands to go into hell, into the fire that never shall be quenched. And if thy foot offend thee, cut it off: it is better for thee to enter halt into life, than having two feet to be cast into hell, into the fire that never shall be quenched. And if thine eye offend thee, pluck it out: it is better for thee to enter into the kingdom of God with one eye, than having two eyes to be cast into hell fire.

—Mark 9:43, 45, 47

Lord, if only all the false gods that lure us were clearly labeled. Forgive us, Lord. Help us to keep even good things in balance and never to pursue anything with more fervor than we pursue our relationship with you.

> **Father, forgive them; for they know
> not what they do.**
>
> —Luke 23:34

God knows that as hard as we may try, there are times when we will make human mistakes. Even so, if we trust in him and ask his forgiveness, he will bless us with mercy and peace.

Verily, verily, I say unto you, Hereafter ye
shall see heaven open, and the angels of God
ascending and descending upon the Son of man.

—John 1:51

Heaven is a fluttering of angels' wings, the uproar
of celestial songs, the clamor of love run loose. What
joyous music to our earthly ears!

> Of a truth I say unto you, that this poor widow hath cast in more than they all: For all these have of their abundance cast in unto the offerings of God: but she of her penury hath cast in all the living that she had.
>
> —Luke 21:3–4

I ask you for a spirit of both generosity and trust. Generosity prompts us to want to share what we have with others, to take care of our neighbors. Trust lets us believe that you will take care of us and provide our daily bread. When I am blessed with abundance, let me give with abundance. And when I feel scarcity, let me give anyway.

Take these things hence; make not my Father's house an house of merchandise.

—John 2:16

Lord, your ways of humility, love, and forgiveness are so at odds with worldly material values that there is no way to play both fields at once. I have a choice to make. Do I choose to indulge in a lifetime of hedonistic pleasures, or will I choose to serve you, walking in your peaceful ways now and looking forward to the promise of eternity? I know what I choose, Lord. That's why I'm spending time with you right now. Help me to walk without compromise today.

A certain man made a great supper, and bade many: And sent his servant at supper time to say to them that were bidden, Come; for all things are now ready. And they all with one consent began to make excuse. The first said unto him, I have bought a piece of ground, and I must needs go and see it: I pray thee have me excused. And another said, I have bought five yoke of oxen, and I go to prove them: I pray thee have me excused. And another said, I have married a wife, and therefore I cannot come. So that servant came, and shewed his lord these things.

—Luke 14:16-21

Help me see the connection between our relationship, O God, and the ones I have with others: my spouse, friends, and children. I use them all as excuses for not praying when they're a prime reason to pray!

Then the master of the house being angry said to his servant, Go out quickly into the streets and lanes of the city, and bring in hither the poor, and the maimed, and the halt, and the blind. And the servant said, Lord, it is done as thou hast commanded, and yet there is room. And the lord said unto the servant, Go out into the highways and hedges, and compel them to come in, that my house may be filled. For I say unto you, That none of those men which were bidden shall taste of my supper.

—Luke 14:21-24

Our tangible gifts to help the poor mirror God's spiritual gifts that keep flowing toward us to meet our needs.

As our hands extend food, clothing, and shelter to those who lack it, God's hands extend grace, mercy, and forgiveness to give us all that our needy souls lack.

> **When Jesus saw their faith, he said unto the sick of the palsy, Son, thy sins be forgiven thee.**
>
> **—Mark 2:5**

Jesus, the man who was sick of the palsy was carried to you by four friends, who very creatively found a way to lower him from the rooftop. Thank you for those friends who carry me to you in prayer when I am at the end of my rope. Help me to be that friend to others.

If ye love me, keep my commandments. And I will pray the Father, and he shall give you another Comforter, that he may abide with you for ever; Even the Spirit of truth; whom the world cannot receive, because it seeth him not, neither knoweth him: but ye know him; for he dwelleth with you, and shall be in you.

—John 14:15-17

I can look over my shoulder and see times when you, Pathfinding God, were a ready and dependable companion. I couldn't have done it without you. And I believe that you are already waiting to take my hand into tomorrow—knowledge that gives me the security to risk.

I am come to send fire on the earth; and what will I, if it be already kindled? But I have a baptism to be baptized with; and how am I straitened till it be accomplished!

—Luke 12:49-50

Lord, you come to us in the storm, the fire, and even in the stillness of a quiet moment. Sometimes your message is strong, carried on bustling angelic wings; sometimes our spirits are nudged, our hearts lightened by the gentle whisper of spirit voices. However you approach us, your message is always one of tender love and compassion. Thank you for the certainty—and the surprise—of your holy voice.

There is no man which shall do a miracle
in my name, that can lightly speak evil of me.
For he that is not against us is on our part. For
whosoever shall give you a cup of water to drink
in my name, because ye belong to Christ, verily I
say unto you, he shall not lose his reward.

—Mark 9:39-41

Lifting others up in prayer is an exercise in faith. When
we extend a hand to help others, we show our devotion
to Jesus.

August

> As thou hast given him power over all flesh,
> that he should give eternal life to as many as
> thou hast given him. And this is life eternal, that
> they might know thee the only true God, and
> Jesus Christ, whom thou hast sent.
>
> —John 17:2-3

O Lord, what a comfort it is to know that you are working to perfect us even on days when we feel anything but perfect. One day all creation will be perfected. How we look forward to that day when our faith is fully realized, and we are complete in you!

> Beware of the scribes, which love to go
> in long clothing, and love salutations in
> the marketplaces, and the chief seats in the
> synagogues, and the uppermost rooms at
> feasts: Which devour widows' houses, and for a
> pretence make long prayers: these shall receive
> greater damnation.
>
> —Mark 12:38-40

Jesus showed us the strength and power of humility, blessing us by his sacrifice.

What is this then that is written, The stone which the builders rejected, the same is become the head of the corner? Whosoever shall fall upon that stone shall be broken; but on whomsoever it shall fall, it will grind him to powder.

—Luke 20:17-18

Give thanks to God, for he is good. Even when we are struggling, God is there to help us. Even when we are feeling lost and alone, God stands beside us and shows us we are loved. Even when we are sure we cannot go on, God picks us up and carries us. Give thanks to God.

> I am come a light into the world, that whosoever believeth on me should not abide in darkness. And if any man hear my words, and believe not, I judge him not: for I came not to judge the world, but to save the world.
>
> —John 12:46-47

God is poised to save all who call on him.

To open their eyes, and to turn them from darkness to light, and from the power of Satan unto God, that they may receive forgiveness of sins, and inheritance among them which are sanctified by faith that is in me.

—Acts 26:18

God's love brightens and beautifies even the darkest days.

> I am: and ye shall see the Son of man sitting on the right hand of power, and coming in the clouds of heaven.
>
> —Mark 14:62

Today I want to praise your name, Jesus. I want to be joyful in a way that spills over, full of awe and thanksgiving. I want to make a sacrifice of praise, to revel in the works of your hands, to delight in your awesome power.

He that believeth on me, the works that I do shall he do also; and greater works than these shall he do; because I go unto my Father. And whatsoever ye shall ask in my name, that will I do, that the Father may be glorified in the Son. If ye shall ask any thing in my name, I will do it.

—John 14:12-14

God Almighty, hear my prayer. Give me wings to soar when my feet get tired. Give me manna from heaven when my stomach growls with hunger. Give me fuel for my spirit when my mood is low. God, hear my prayer!

> Whereunto then shall I liken the men of this generation? and to what are they like? They are like unto children sitting in the marketplace, and calling one to another, and saying, We have piped unto you, and ye have not danced; we have mourned to you, and ye have not wept.
>
> —Luke 7:31-32

When I am thankful for what I have, I am given more. When I am not thankful, what I have is taken away. Gratitude is like a door that, when opened, leads to even more good things. But to be ungrateful keeps that door closed, and keeps me away from what God wants to bless me with. I am thankful, always.

> A prophet is not without honour,
> but in his own country, and among his own kin,
> and in his own house.
>
> —Mark 6:4

When I am feeling uncertain and alone, I can turn to the Scriptures. The prophets often felt unworthy of their call. Hannah felt alone in her barrenness. Jesus himself cried out on the cross, quoting Psalm 22, asking why God had forsaken him. But God's love reached all of them.

> Ye have heard that it was said of them of old time, Thou shalt not kill; and whosoever shall kill shall be in danger of the judgment: But I say unto you, That whosoever is angry with his brother without a cause shall be in danger of the judgment: and whosoever shall say to his brother, Raca, shall be in danger of the council: but whosoever shall say, Thou fool, shall be in danger of hell fire.
>
> —Matthew 5:21-22

Once that verbal barb is out there, there's no taking it back. It may have felt good for a moment, but the sense of triumph gives way almost immediately to a sense of regret. If wisdom rules our tongues, however, the sword of our words will defend and encourage those around us. It will secure honor and blessing by its careful use and make those around us feel secure rather than threatened.

> **He that is not with me is against me: and he that gathereth not with me scattereth.**
>
> —Luke 11:23

I can't make a blade of grass grow, Lord. By contrast, you created this entire universe and all it contains. If that doesn't inspire worship in my soul, I can't imagine what will. But the truth is that it does put me in awe of you; it does stir my heart to join in the worship of your kingdom of heaven.

> **Verily I say unto you, One of you which eateth with me shall betray me.**
>
> —Mark 14:18

Lord, I know it is your will for us to forgive those who do us wrong, and I know that once we do, everything goes so much more smoothly in our lives. We forgive because you first forgave us, and I'm starting to understand that. Help me to forgive, Lord. Take away the hurt and betrayal, and leave only your peace.

Remember the word that I said unto you, The servant is not greater than his lord. If they have persecuted me, they will also persecute you; if they have kept my saying, they will keep yours also. But all these things will they do unto you for my name's sake, because they know not him that sent me. If I had not come and spoken unto them, they had not had sin: but now they have no cloak for their sin.

—John 15:20-22

We will know when it's time to make our stand. God will speak to us a little louder, a little stronger. The whisper within will become a mighty roar, as we are encouraged to step out in faith and be who God meant us to be.

My head with oil thou didst not anoint:
but this woman hath anointed my feet with
ointment. Wherefore I say unto thee, Her sins,
which are many, are forgiven; for she loved
much: but to whom little is forgiven, the same
loveth little.

—Luke 7:46–47

Let me be as extravagant in my love for you, Jesus, as the woman who anointed your feet with oil. Let me freely admit my sins, and my debt to you, so that I may be forgiven.

> **With men it is impossible, but not with God:**
> **for with God all things are possible.**
>
> —Mark 10:27

When all seems lost and you want to stop, remember God made you to shine and be epic! Small hearts give up, but you have the heart of a lion. Know that with God all things are possible. Keep on keepin' on and let the lion within you roar!

> **Whatsoever ye shall ask the Father in my name, he will give it you.**
>
> —John 16:23

Lord, if all the prayers ever prayed were linked together, surely they would reach to heaven and back countless times! We want to be a people who pray without ceasing, Lord. Hear both the prayers we utter and the silent prayers of our hearts, and may you also sense how grateful we are to serve a God who listens to our prayers and sends us his answers.

Which of you shall have a friend, and shall go unto him at midnight, and say unto him, Friend, lend me three loaves; For a friend of mine in his journey is come to me, and I have nothing to set before him? And he from within shall answer and say, Trouble me not: the door is now shut, and my children are with me in bed; I cannot rise and give thee. I say unto you, Though he will not rise and give him, because he is his friend, yet because of his importunity he will rise and give him as many as he needeth.

—Luke 11:5-8

As someone who has a hard time waiting for the microwave to heat my lunch, waiting for your answers to prayer is excruciating. But I've come to see that these waiting periods are good for me. I grow in discipline, and discover the peace of your presence.

It is not for you to know the times or the seasons, which the Father hath put in his own power. But ye shall receive power, after that the Holy Ghost is come upon you: and ye shall be witnesses unto me both in Jerusalem, and in all Judaea, and in Samaria, and unto the uttermost part of the earth.

—Acts 1:7-8

Isn't it amazing how just trusting in God's power and grace can heal us? See it, know it, and heal it. What a gift we have been given!

Full well ye reject the commandment of God, that ye may keep your own tradition. For Moses said, Honour thy father and thy mother; and, Whoso curseth father or mother, let him die the death: But ye say, If a man shall say to his father or mother, It is Corban, that is to say, a gift, by whatsoever thou mightest be profited by me; he shall be free. And ye suffer him no more to do ought for his father or his mother; Making the word of God of none effect through your tradition, which ye have delivered: and many such like things do ye.

—Mark 7:9-13

So often I am inclined to brush away criticism and say, "this is the way it's always been." Lord, help me to value your Word over the practices I've adopted in my life, no matter how permanent they may seem.

> My time is not yet come: but your time is
> alway ready. The world cannot hate you;
> but me it hateth, because I testify of it, that the
> works thereof are evil. Go ye up unto this feast:
> I go not up yet unto this feast; for my time is
> not yet full come.
>
> —John 7:6-8

O Lord, your gift of love is often distorted in this world of ours. You are the source of the only perfect love we will ever know. Thank you, Lord, for abiding in us

and helping us love ourselves and others. On this day, Lord, I pray that you will draw near to anyone who is feeling unloved. May they accept your unconditional love so they will know what true love is!

He that knew not, and did commit things worthy of stripes, shall be beaten with few stripes. For unto whomsoever much is given, of him shall be much required: and to whom men have committed much, of him they will ask the more.

—Luke 12:48

Lord, help me to depend on you to be my source of goodness. I don't always feel like being patient, kind, loving, or joyful, but you are all of these things by your very nature. So right now I place my strengths and weaknesses into your hands, asking you to infuse them with yourself and to make them instruments of good that will serve others for your sake.

> Verily, verily, I say unto you, Whosoever committeth sin is the servant of sin. And the servant abideth not in the house for ever: but the Son abideth ever. If the Son therefore shall make you free, ye shall be free indeed.
>
> —John 8:34-36

Lord, when we look back and remember all the ways you've guided us in the past, we know we have no need to be anxious about the future. You were, are, and always will be our Savior and Lord. Why should we fear instability when you are always here with us?

> **Repent: for the kingdom of
> heaven is at hand.**
>
> **—Matthew 4:17**

Lord, I never want to think about my failures. But I know I need to acknowledge my sins—not to wallow in guilt, but to repent and then let go of them. Thank you for holding out your arms in forgiveness. It is a gift, that you know my shortcomings and love me anyway. You want me to repent so that you can welcome me into your kingdom of heaven!

> **Judge not, and ye shall not be judged: condemn not, and ye shall not be condemned: forgive, and ye shall be forgiven: Give, and it shall be given unto you; good measure, pressed down, and shaken together, and running over, shall men give into your bosom. For with the same measure that ye mete withal it shall be measured to you again.**
>
> **—Luke 6:37-38**

Why is it often the people closest to us that hurt us the most? Today I ask for the strength to deal with difficult people in the way you would want me to: to forgive them their trespasses, as I would hope they'd forgive mine. Today I ask for enough love to look beyond their problems and see them as you see them, as human beings deserving of love and care. Help me to forgive and move on, God. Amen.

It is written in the prophets, And they shall be all taught of God. Every man therefore that hath heard, and hath learned of the Father, cometh unto me. Not that any man hath seen the Father, save he which is of God, he hath seen the Father.

—John 6:45-46

Imagine having the arms of a loving, caring angel wrapped around you when you are sad or upset. Faith is like that. Comforting and encouraging, faith is like a trustworthy old friend that is never too tired or busy to hear your problems or help you find your footing again when you stumble through life. Faith in God is our best friend and ally.

> **Take heed, and beware of covetousness:**
> **for a man's life consisteth not in the abundance**
> **of the things which he possesseth.**
>
> **—Luke 12:15**

Father, you've shown me that coveting isn't always as straightforward as wishing I had someone else's house or car. The covetous corruption that creeps in can wear any number of disguises, such as despising someone else's success or hoping for their failure so I won't feel left behind. Set me free today to enjoy the blessings you've provided without pointless comparisons.

In the world ye shall have tribulation: but be of good cheer; I have overcome the world.

—John 16:33

Give me peace of mind today, for I am worried about so many things. Give me peace of heart today, for I am fearful of challenges before me. Give me peace of spirit today, for I am in a state of confusion and chaos. I ask, God, for your peace today, and every day, to help keep my feet on the right path and my faith solid and unmoving. Without peace, I don't see the answers you place before me. Without peace, I cannot hear your still, small voice within. Shower me today with your loving peace, God, and all will be well in my mind, heart, and spirit. Amen.

> Go ye, and tell that fox, Behold, I cast out
> devils, and I do cures to day and to morrow, and
> the third day I shall be perfected. Nevertheless
> I must walk to day, and to morrow, and the day
> following: for it cannot be that a prophet perish
> out of Jerusalem.
>
> —Luke 13:32-33

Lord, I need you here in the midst of this difficult
situation, that the very warmth of your love will bring
about the resolution and that the brightness of your
light will cast out all shadows between us. Amen.

O Jerusalem, Jerusalem, which killest the prophets, and stonest them that are sent unto thee; how often would I have gathered thy children together, as a hen doth gather her brood under her wings, and ye would not! Behold, your house is left unto you desolate: and verily I say unto you, Ye shall not see me, until the time come when ye shall say, Blessed is he that cometh in the name of the Lord.

—Luke 13:34-35

Lord, I pray I will stop taking all your miraculous works for granted. Whether I praise you through song, words, or actions, I want to praise you not only for what you are doing, but also for all you have done in the past. Help me see the holiness of the ordinary in each day.

Be not afraid, only believe.

—Mark 5:36

Lord, it is sometimes hard to love those around me when they are so different in their beliefs and behaviors. I find myself sometimes feeling intolerant, even afraid. But you gave me the commandment to love others as myself, and that if I love you, then I love all of your creation. Help me to open my heart and my mind to those I see as being different, and find in them the common light of your presence. Help me to be a better person and not fear others just because they are not like me. Help me to see the wonder and magic in learning about others and letting them learn about me.

What woman having ten pieces of silver, if she lose one piece, doth not light a candle, and sweep the house, and seek diligently till she find it? And when she hath found it, she calleth her friends and her neighbours together, saying, Rejoice with me; for I have found the piece which I had lost.

—Luke 15:8-9

There is great joy when lost things are found— lost lambs, lost coins, but especially lost people. Sometimes we lose our joy, like the older brother in the story of the prodigal son. The good news is that we can turn to God and find it again.

September

As the Father hath loved me, so have I loved you: continue ye in my love. If ye keep my commandments, ye shall abide in my love; even as I have kept my Father's commandments, and abide in his love. These things have I spoken unto you, that my joy might remain in you, and that your joy might be full.

—John 15:9-11

Dear Lord, in this time of back-to-school excitement, I pray for all children who are returning to the classroom. May they have a productive year of education and friendship. Please grant teachers patience and fulfillment, and bless all maintenance workers, administrators, principals, and aides who work behind the scenes. I pray especially for those who are apprehensive about this return—non-traditional learners, children who are being bullied, and children and staff who are dealing with weighty issues at home. May they feel your presence each school day.

> **Forbid him not:**
> **for he that is not against us is for us.**
>
> **—Luke 9:50**

Like it or not, we affect others by what we say and do. Whether with friends, family, coworkers, or even total strangers, God wants us to always treat others with the utmost care and respect.

Ye have not chosen me, but I have chosen you, and ordained you, that ye should go and bring forth fruit, and that your fruit should remain: that whatsoever ye shall ask of the Father in my name, he may give it you. These things I command you, that ye love one another.

—John 15:16-17

We are naturally drawn to beautiful, kind, loving people. Mature love knows how to love those who seem unlovable, those who seem incapable of giving us anything in return for our love. This kind of love is heaven's love.

> **Thy faith hath made thee whole; go in peace.**
>
> **—Mark 5:34**

Your peace is like the sweet calm air after a storm, like a happy smile of someone I love on a day when nothing has gone right. Your peace brings me the comfort and the strength I need to get through the hardest of times and the thickest of situations. I am so grateful, God, for the kind of peace your presence offers me, a peace so deep and abiding I know that no matter what is happening, that peace is there for me to tap into.

Like an overflowing well at the center of my being, your presence is the water that quenches my thirst and gives me renewed vigor and life. Thank you, God, for your everlasting peace. Amen.

I know thy works, and tribulation, and
poverty, (but thou art rich).

—Revelation 2:9

Just because God's way of helping us is different than
what we hoped or expected, it doesn't mean he is
indifferent to our cries for help. We must believe that
he knows what is truly best for us and is actively doing
what is best for us.

The ground of a certain rich man brought forth plentifully: And he thought within himself, saying, What shall I do, because I have no room where to bestow my fruits? And he said, This will I do: I will pull down my barns, and build greater; and there will I bestow all my fruits and my goods. And I will say to my soul, Soul, thou hast much goods laid up for many years; take thine ease, eat, drink, and be merry.

—Luke 12:16-19

Father God, all of our resources and all we have came from you, and they are only ours for a little while. Protect us from any addiction to material things, Lord. Gently remind us when we have enough—enough to eat, enough to wear, enough to enjoy. Most of all, keep us mindful of the fact that because we have you, we have everything we need.

> But God said unto him, Thou fool, this night thy soul shall be required of thee: then whose shall those things be, which thou hast provided? So is he that layeth up treasure for himself, and is not rich toward God.
>
> —Luke 12:20-21

Lord, when in life my own "ground" brings forth plentifully and I am surrounded by the fruits of all my belongings, I call to you. Do not let my judgment be clouded by material things. I trust in you to keep my soul humble and charitable during my fleeting time on this Earth. Remind me of what matters most.

September 8

> **If thou knewest the gift of God, and who it is that saith to thee, Give me to drink; thou wouldest have asked of him, and he would have given thee living water.**
>
> **—John 4:10**

The grace of the living God refreshes like cool, clear water on a hot day, giving our parched souls the sustenance and nourishment they need.

> No man can enter into a strong man's house,
> and spoil his goods, except he will first bind the
> strong man; and then he will spoil his house.
>
> —Mark 3:27

I ask in prayer today for courage and strength to face some big challenges before me. I admit I am anxious, and even afraid, but I know in my heart you will never give me anything I cannot handle, and that you will be by my side the whole way. Instill in me a strong heart and spirit as I deal with my problems and keep my mind centered and focused on the solutions you set before me. I thank you, Lord, for always being there for me in my times of need and struggle. Amen.

September 10

> But even the very hairs of your head are all numbered. Fear not therefore: ye are of more value than many sparrows.
>
> —Luke 12:7

Heavenly Father, I hold up to you my child who is ill. While I think everything will be okay, I worry, and lack of sleep and stress only exacerbate that worry. I know, though, that you love my child even more than I do—even if that seems impossible to me! You want what's best for all of us. During this dark and restless and feverish night, help me let go of my fear as I place my trust and my hope in you.

> And when ye shall hear of wars and rumours of wars, be ye not troubled: for such things must needs be; but the end shall not be yet. For nation shall rise against nation, and kingdom against kingdom: and there shall be earthquakes in divers places, and there shall be famines and troubles: these are the beginnings of sorrows.
>
> —Mark 13:7-8

This is a sad and solemn day, yet there is still time to be thankful. Thank you, Lord, for all the emergency workers who help people every day. They bring light to the darkness and help to those who need it

most. Thank you for their selflessness and willingness to give everything they have to save another. Just as Jesus sacrificed his life to save us, we are blessed by the sacrifices of those who save our lives.

> **Blessed are they that mourn:**
> **for they shall be comforted.**
>
> **—Matthew 5:4**

When I drift away from you, it is often sorrow and need that draw me back. In times of crisis, I instinctively turn towards you. Thank you for sending your Spirit of consolation. Let me always remember that gratitude.

When once the master of the house is risen up, and hath shut to the door, and ye begin to stand without, and to knock at the door, saying, Lord, Lord, open unto us; and he shall answer and say unto you, I know you not whence ye are: Then shall ye begin to say, We have eaten and drunk in thy presence, and thou hast taught in our streets. But he shall say, I tell you, I know you not whence ye are; depart from me, all ye workers of iniquity.

—Luke 13:25-27

Our salvation is not in deeds, but good deeds can't help but flow from the saved.

Verily, verily, I say unto you, Except a corn of wheat fall into the ground and die, it abideth alone: but if it die, it bringeth forth much fruit. He that loveth his life shall lose it; and he that hateth his life in this world shall keep it unto life eternal. If any man serve me, let him follow me; and where I am, there shall also my servant be: if any man serve me, him will my Father honour.

—John 12:24-26

Thank you, Lord, at the harvest time. Thank you for the plants that grow to give us food and thank you for the people who grow them. The Earth's bounty is a miracle! As I enjoy fresh food, may I always be grateful for what I eat and the nutrition it provides.

Take heed to yourselves, lest at any time your hearts be overcharged with surfeiting, and drunkenness, and cares of this life, and so that day come upon you unawares. For as a snare shall it come on all them that dwell on the face of the whole earth. Watch ye therefore, and pray always, that ye may be accounted worthy to escape all these things that shall come to pass, and to stand before the Son of man.

—Luke 21:34-36

If we could stop pretending to be strong and start being honest with ourselves and God, crying out, "God, please help! I am poor and needy," he would hurry to help us and be the strength of our lives.

> **This sickness is not unto death, but for the glory of God, that the Son of God might be glorified thereby.**
>
> —John 11:4

Illness has come like a thief in the night and stolen the innocence of daily, take-it-for-granted life. In God's hands, it can become an opportunity for renewal and discovering what—and who—really matters.

Arise, and take up thy bed, and go thy way into thine house.

—Mark 2:11

Lord, just when I was thinking I was too pooped to get through the day, I heard a praise song on the radio. It reminded me of the unending supply of energy and strength that is ours through faith in you! Thanks for getting me through the day today, Lord. I would be so lost without you.

Now do ye Pharisees make clean the outside of the cup and the platter; but your inward part is full of ravening and wickedness. Ye fools, did not he that made that which is without make that which is within also? But rather give alms of such things as ye have; and, behold, all things are clean unto you.

—Luke 11:39-41

Faith is knowing that you cannot always control what goes on outside of you, but you can always control what goes on inside. Faith is letting go and letting God help see you through.

But woe unto you, Pharisees! for ye tithe mint and rue and all manner of herbs, and pass over judgment and the love of God: these ought ye to have done, and not to leave the other undone. Woe unto you, Pharisees! for ye love the uppermost seats in the synagogues, and greetings in the markets. Woe unto you, scribes and Pharisees, hypocrites! for ye are as graves which appear not, and the men that walk over them are not aware of them.

—Luke 11:42-44

Each of us has the potential for goodness. But focusing on maintaining outward appearances often leaves room for toxicity and rot to fester on the inside. What kind of reputation does this build for us? Lord, protect me from the false and hypocritical.

> **The harvest truly is plenteous, but the labourers are few; Pray ye therefore the Lord of the harvest, that he will send forth labourers into his harvest.**
>
> **—Matthew 9:37-38**

Ready or not, free time is at hand for some of your finest seasoned workers, Lord, early retirees downsized, out-sized, and put prematurely out to pasture. Help us start again, for we are hidden treasures other companies could use. Remind us as we start the search that even temporary employment is better than sitting around. Keep us in the workforce, for we, like fine furniture, gain luster with age, something young folks can't begin to match.

The hour cometh, and now is, when the true worshippers shall worship the Father in spirit and in truth: for the Father seeketh such to worship him. God is a Spirit: and they that worship him must worship him in spirit and in truth.

—John 4:23-24

What would it be like to soar in heaven? What would it be like to worship as naturally as you breathe? What would it be like to dance in the light of God? Hold that thought as long as you can.

> **Fear not: believe only, and she
> shall be made whole.**
>
> —**Luke 8:50**

Lord, I see you in the beauty of the autumn season. Thank you for the brilliant colors of the trees. Thank you for the crisp, cool air that refreshes me. I am blessed to see autumn's beauty everywhere I go. Thank you for showing me that a time of change can be one of the most gorgeous seasons on Earth.

Jesus said unto them, Ye know not what ye ask: can ye drink of the cup that I drink of? and be baptized with the baptism that I am baptized with? And they said unto him, We can. And Jesus said unto them, Ye shall indeed drink of the cup that I drink of; and with the baptism that I am baptized withal shall ye be baptized.

—Mark 10:38-39

When I walk with God, I become stronger and wiser each day. No obstacle can delay me. No challenge can destroy me. When I move in God's will, no difficulty can defeat me. When I heed God's word, no goal can elude me!

> **If any man will come after me,**
> **let him deny himself, and take up his cross daily,**
> **and follow me.**
>
> —**Luke 9:23**

If I remain small, whom do I serve? Certainly not God, who created me to be big and bold and authentic. Certainly not the world, which needs my creative fire and loving spirit. Certainly not myself, with so much to live for and offer. Let me be big, bold, and authentic!

> Behold, the devil shall cast some of you into prison, that ye may be tried; and ye shall have tribulation ten days: be thou faithful unto death, and I will give thee a crown of life.
>
> —**Revelation 2:10**

Lord, when I see anger and strife around me, it's difficult to keep my own equilibrium and trust in you. I try to have faith that "all things work together for good to them that love God" (Romans 8:28), but my faith does falter. When I'm surrounded by division, let me be rooted in faith, unshaken by the passing concerns of this world. Let me be a person of peace myself—not false peace, that ignores problems that need to be addressed—but the true peace that comes from you.

> The Son of man is come eating and drinking; and ye say, Behold a gluttonous man, and a winebibber, a friend of publicans and sinners! But wisdom is justified of all her children.
>
> —Luke 7:34-35

Thank you, Lord, for teachers. How can I ever repay the men and women who taught me and opened my eyes to the world? How can I ever truly thank the people who teach my children and guide them on their journey through life? I am so grateful for those who teach and mentor. Thank you for giving us knowledge and wisdom to carry on life's path.

Jesus answered and said unto him, What wilt thou that I should do unto thee? The blind man said unto him, Lord, that I might receive my sight. And Jesus said unto him, Go thy way; thy faith hath made thee whole.

—Mark 10:51-52

Thank God when the pain ends, when once again we're well and whole and strong. Thank God when our bodies are released from the blinding, mind-numbing hurts that affect our whole lives. Thank God when we have complete victory over pain.

> **Are there not twelve hours in the day? If any man walk in the day, he stumbleth not, because he seeth the light of this world. But if a man walk in the night, he stumbleth, because there is no light in him.**
>
> **—John 11:9-10**

Dear God, I look around and see so many people hurting one another, and it makes my heart heavy and sad. I pray for a way to walk through this world without drowning in sorrow and defeat. I pray for a light to focus upon when all I hear and see is dark and bleak. Help me, God, to focus on the beauty and wonder the world has to offer. Help me recognize the good and the kind and the loving. I pray to see beyond my sadness and despair, and to not let my disappointment overshadow my hope. Amen.

Jesus answering said unto him, Simon, I have somewhat to say unto thee. And he saith, Master, say on. There was a certain creditor which had two debtors: the one owed five hundred pence, and the other fifty. And when they had nothing to pay, he frankly forgave them both. Tell me therefore, which of them will love him most? Simon answered and said, I suppose that he, to whom he forgave most. And he said unto him, Thou hast rightly judged.

—Luke 7:40-43

Have you ever been overwhelmed with gratitude toward God? That's the work of God's Spirit in us, filling us with praise, thanks, and love. These are precious offerings held in God's treasury of remembrance, just as we hold our own children's love gifts close to our hearts.

> **The time is fulfilled, and the kingdom of God is at hand: repent ye, and believe the gospel.**
>
> **—Mark 1:15**

I ask in prayer for your forgiveness. I've not been the most loving and kind person lately, and I've treated people terribly as a result. I plan to reach out to each and every one of them and ask their forgiveness, but first I come to you in hopes that you will help me be a better person, a more loving and caring friend, and someone who treats others as I'd like to be treated. Please take away the defects in me that cause me to do harm to others, and strengthen the good qualities I have. Please forgive me and empower me to make better choices in the future and to be the person you want me to be. Amen.

October

> **Be of good cheer: it is I; be not afraid.**
>
> **—Mark 6:50**

Fall is a time of change. Sometimes that change is beautiful, as when the leaves begin to change color. Sometimes that change brings loss, as the days grow shorter and the trees grow bare. Let me never be afraid to change and grow myself—and let me remember that you are with me even in times of loss and sorrow.

Behold, I give unto you power to tread on
serpents and scorpions, and over all the
power of the enemy: and nothing shall by
any means hurt you. Notwithstanding in this
rejoice not, that the spirits are subject unto you;
but rather rejoice, because your names
are written in heaven.

—Luke 10:19-20

Oh Lord, when I see
terrible, fearful events—
explosions destroying
whole buildings,
droughts that turn
crops to dust, storms
devastating all in their
path—I turn to you.
You are always here,
listening, caring, and
waiting for all of us to
reach out to you. Amen.

I am the resurrection, and the life: he that believeth in me, though he were dead, yet shall he live: And whosoever liveth and believeth in me shall never die. Believest thou this?

—John 11:25-26

My God is an awesome God, for he not only loves me, he empowers me to strive to be the best I can be every day. I am always provided with new opportunities to shine, as long as I hold fast to my faith in him, and listen for his guidance.

If ye love them which love you, what thank
have ye? for sinners also love those that love
them. And if ye do good to them which do good
to you, what thank have ye? for sinners also do
even the same. And if ye lend to them of whom
ye hope to receive, what thank have ye? for
sinners also lend to sinners, to receive as
much again.

—Luke 6:32-34

Our strengths were
given to us to help us
serve. God rejoices when
we change our "How
can I help myself?"
attitude to one of "How
can I help others?"

October 5

> **Rejoice, and be exceeding glad: for great is your reward in heaven: for so persecuted they the prophets which were before you.**
>
> —Matthew 5:12

When my courage wavers, when it would be difficult to witness to my faith, let me be inspired by the faith of those who came before me. Hold me fast to my convictions, God, so I may honor you and not stray from your path.

If the world hate you, ye know that it hated me before it hated you. If ye were of the world, the world would love his own: but because ye are not of the world, but I have chosen you out of the world, therefore the world hateth you.

—John 15:18-19

Today I feel alone, yet I am not lonely. There is peace in solitude and rejuvenation in the quiet of being alone. Lead my thoughts to restful healing, Lord. Help me

use this time alone to find myself and reach deep inside my heart and mind to discover peace. I rejoice in being away from the noise and clatter of everyday life and praise God for letting me have this time for myself.

For which of you, intending to build a tower, sitteth not down first, and counteth the cost, whether he have sufficient to finish it? Lest haply, after he hath laid the foundation, and is not able to finish it, all that behold it begin to mock him, Saying, This man began to build, and was not able to finish.

—Luke 14:28-30

Dear God, I long to change parts of my life that are no longer working, but don't know where to start. Help me break down these big, scary goals into small and achievable steps. Give me courage to put these plans into action and turn my life around!

Or what king, going to make war against another king, sitteth not down first, and consulteth whether he be able with ten thousand to meet him that cometh against him with twenty thousand? Or else, while the other is yet a great way off, he sendeth an ambassage, and desireth conditions of peace. So likewise, whosoever he be of you that forsaketh not all that he hath, he cannot be my disciple.

—Luke 14:31-33

We know, Lord, that action is the proper fruit of knowledge and all spiritual insight. But so often we wish only to think and muse, without ever doing good toward anyone. Help us to forsake the ease and comfort of a purposeless life.

If ye were blind, ye should have no sin: but now ye say, We see; therefore your sin remaineth.

—John 9:41

The wisdom and insight we need is often hidden in plain sight, right before our eyes, and under our very noses. God is always guiding us, if we stop and open our hearts and spirits to the still, small whisperings within that point the way.

Why reason ye these things in your hearts?
Whether is it easier to say to the sick of the
palsy, Thy sins be forgiven thee; or to say, Arise,
and take up thy bed, and walk?

—Mark 2:8-9

The miracle of God's presence is the vision I keep my focus on, so that I am always striving to be better as a person and a positive force for change. Even when times are tough, that vision stays true, and I keep moving towards its completion.

Come unto me, all ye that labour and are heavy laden, and I will give you rest. Take my yoke upon you, and learn of me; for I am meek and lowly in heart: and ye shall find rest unto your souls. For my yoke is easy, and my burden is light.

—Matthew 11:28-30

Lord, help them, comfort them, and bring them peace and sweet, pain-free sleep. Ease the tension in their bodies and the ache in their hearts. Heal their hurts, please, Lord, and let them rest easy.

If ye had faith as a grain of mustard seed,
ye might say unto this sycamine tree, Be thou
plucked up by the root, and be thou planted in
the sea; and it should obey you.

—Luke 17:6

When trouble strikes, O God, we are restored by small signs of hope found in ordinary places: friends, random kindness, shared pain, and support. Help us collect them like mustard seeds that can grow into a spreading harvest of well-being.

I have given them thy word; and the world hath hated them, because they are not of the world, even as I am not of the world.

—John 17:14

It is easy to have self-pity and resent the painful trials and heartaches that come into our lives. But God always works for our greater good.

I pray not that thou shouldest take them out of the world, but that thou shouldest keep them from the evil.

—John 17:15

Heavenly Father, I ask for your healing presence. Protect me from the worldly hurts and evil that have clouded my life and robbed me of joy. Help me forget the past, to let go of grudges, and to make a new start. Take away the darkness of my sorrow, and flood it with the light of your love. Forgive me, so I might forgive others. Amen.

> The fearful, and unbelieving, and the abominable, and murderers, and whoremongers, and sorcerers, and idolaters, and all liars, shall have their part in the lake which burneth with fire and brimstone: which is the second death.
>
> —Revelation 21:8

You are ultimately the one who permits nations and rulers to rise and fall, Lord. You alone are the King of Kings, and you do all things well—with righteousness, justice, and truth. When all is said and done, you won't allow evil to prevail. Indeed, all people—whether powerful or peasant, rich or poor—will be called to give you an account of how they've lived. In light of that, help me to live well today, honoring you in all I do.

Beware ye of the leaven of the Pharisees, which is hypocrisy. For there is nothing covered, that shall not be revealed; neither hid, that shall not be known. Therefore whatsoever ye have spoken in darkness shall be heard in the light; and that which ye have spoken in the ear in closets shall be proclaimed upon the housetops.

—Luke 12:1-3

It's hard, Lord, to reveal my heart to you, though it's the thing I most want to do. Remind me in this dialogue that you already know what is within me. You wait—O thank you!—hoping for the gift of my willingness to acknowledge the good you already see and the bad you've long forgotten and forgiven.

Have ye never read what David did, when he had need, and was an hungred, he, and they that were with him? How he went into the house of God in the days of Abiathar the high priest, and did eat the shewbread, which is not lawful to eat but for the priests, and gave also to them which were with him?

—Mark 2:25-26

O God, I am guilty of transgressions that make me ashamed, and I fear you'll leave me. Yet have you ever refused to forgive those who ask? Why would I be different? Reassured, I accept forgiveness and will share it with those who need it from me.

> This day is salvation come to this house, forsomuch as he also is a son of Abraham. For the Son of man is come to seek and to save that which was lost.
>
> —Luke 19:9-10

All I have to do is take the first step and God will meet me there. Together, we will walk the path and meet every challenge with courage. Together, we will find miracles waiting around every corner. Just one step...

October 19

Take, eat: this is my body.

—Mark 14:22

Thank you for sustaining food, from plain oatmeal for everyday breakfasts to exquisite chocolates for special occasions. Thank you for shared meals with family and friends, where we also share what's going on in our lives. Whatever we eat, ultimately it is your love for us that sustains us.

This is my blood of the new testament, which is shed for many. Verily I say unto you, I will drink no more of the fruit of the vine, until that day that I drink it new in the kingdom of God.

—Mark 14:24-25

Lord of my heart, give me a refreshing drink from the fountains of your love, walking through this desert as I have. Lord of my heart, spread out before me a new vision of your goodness, locked into this dull routine as I was. Lord of my heart, lift up a shining awareness of your will and purpose, awash in doubts and fears though I be.

> **The hour is come, that the Son of man should be glorified.**
>
> —John 12:23

Thank you, Lord, for signs of your power. Thank you for the awe I feel during a thunderstorm or at the sight of a monument in nature. Thank you for the thrill I feel when I see one of your works in all its glory. It is good to know your power and feel its presence in my life.

> When they had found him, they said unto him, All men seek for thee. And he said unto them, Let us go into the next towns, that I may preach there also: for therefore came I forth.
>
> —Mark 1:37–38

Jesus had to balance the need for private prayer and public ministry. So do those of us who follow him! Time spent alone with God renews us spiritually, but we are also called to share God's word and God's love with others. If we're feeling drained and irritated, it may be pointing us towards a spiritual need to be fulfilled. If we're feeling anxious or restless in our prayer lives, it may be because we have ample energy that's not being carried outward.

Can the blind lead the blind? shall they not both fall into the ditch? The disciple is not above his master: but every one that is perfect shall be as his master.

—Luke 6:39-40

Lord, teaching others can uplift and inspire! Help me to share with others what I know; help me to be a strong, wise teacher.

He that hateth me hateth my Father also. If I had not done among them the works which none other man did, they had not had sin: but now have they both seen and hated both me and my Father. But this cometh to pass, that the word might be fulfilled that is written in their law, They hated me without a cause.

—John 15:23-25

I don't come in prayer to you to ask for total forgiveness, even though I know you do forgive me my sins and mistakes. I ask that in addition to your merciful grace, you also help me to learn from my experience and

glean wisdom from my interactions with the people I need to forgive, or need forgiveness from. Without this understanding, I fear I will repeat the same patterns in the future.

Ye are they which justify yourselves before men; but God knoweth your hearts: for that which is highly esteemed among men is abomination in the sight of God. The law and the prophets were until John: since that time the kingdom of God is preached, and every man presseth into it. And it is easier for heaven and earth to pass, than one tittle of the law to fail.

—Luke 16:15-17

It isn't necessary to pray in order for God to know what's on our minds—he already knows. We pray so we will know what's on God's mind.

> The hour is coming, and now is, when the dead shall hear the voice of the Son of God: and they that hear shall live. For as the Father hath life in himself; so hath he given to the Son to have life in himself; And hath given him authority to execute judgment also, because he is the Son of man.
>
> —John 5:25-27

Lord, you know how all-encompassing grief can be. Thank you, Lord, for bringing us comfort during such times. Eventually the day comes when we have the pleasant realization that we actually feel a little

invigorated. We hold our heads a little higher as you help us find joy in our memories and peace in the knowledge that our loved one is safe by your side, looking down on us over your shoulder.

October 27

> Marvel not at this: for the hour is coming, in the which all that are in the graves shall hear his voice, And shall come forth; they that have done good, unto the resurrection of life; and they that have done evil, unto the resurrection of damnation.
>
> —John 5:28-29

Death is not an end to be feared and dreaded for those who love the Lord.

> Now the brother shall betray the brother to death, and the father the son; and children shall rise up against their parents, and shall cause them to be put to death. And ye shall be hated of all men for my name's sake: but he that shall endure unto the end, the same shall be saved.
>
> —Mark 13:12-13

Hearts frozen by betrayal can be thawed by the touch of God, who brings to life what at first looks hopeless.

October 29

> Woe unto you, lawyers! for ye have taken away the key of knowledge: ye entered not in yourselves, and them that were entering in ye hindered.
>
> —Luke 11:52

Lord, why is it that frustration sometimes turns to despair and self-destruction? There are so many destructive forces in the world as it is, why do I sometimes make a bad situation worse because of my bitter attitude? How often I wish I could take back thoughtless, hurtful words I have said to a loved one during the course of a trying day. How many times I wish I could have a "do over." But there are no "do overs" in real life. Help me to make amends and handle things better the next time I am challenged.

> **Why sleep ye? rise and pray,**
> **lest ye enter into temptation.**
>
> **—Luke 22:46**

Maybe it's bitterness. Maybe it's timidity. Maybe it's pride. Or maybe we tend to gossip or complain. Whatever sins we struggle with, though, we should never lose heart! Often it's our weaknesses that keep us close to God. When we find ourselves overwhelmed with feelings of bitterness, it's a signal that we're not devoting enough time to prayer and reflection. God is faithful, and it's only through him that we can overcome our weaknesses. So rather than becoming discouraged that we still suffer under the same old struggles, we need to look at our struggles as strings binding us to our heavenly Father.

> **Thou savourest not the things that be of God,**
> **but the things that be of men.**
>
> **—Mark 8:33**

Happy Halloween! Even though Halloween is built around fear, it can also be a time of joy and gratitude. Thank you for the joy I feel when I see children dressed in costume and enjoying their special night. Thank you for a day when everyone can be as weird as they want to be. Thank you for letting us celebrate the unusual and see the world in a different way.

November

November 1

Father, I will that they also, whom thou hast given me, be with me where I am; that they may behold my glory, which thou hast given me: for thou lovedst me before the foundation of the world.

—John 17:24

O Lord, as we enter this season of thanksgiving, how important it is for us to grasp the concept of "enough." You know how this world tempts us with all that is bigger, better—more in every way! But there is such joy and freedom in trusting that you will give us exactly what we need—neither too little nor too much. May we never take for granted all the blessings we have, Lord, and may we be as generous with others as you are with us. It is the simple life that brings us closest to you; we are blessed when we live simply.

> **When the Lord saw her, he had compassion on her, and said unto her, Weep not. And he came and touched the bier: and they that bare him stood still. And he said, Young man, I say unto thee, Arise.**
>
> **—Luke 7:13–14**

The widow whose only son died didn't even need to ask Jesus for help. When he saw her desperate grief, he reached out to perform a miracle. I can only imagine her incredulous joy, and how startled and amazed all the mourners must have been.

Those who were bearing the bier must have seen something in this stranger who came to them, that they halted when Jesus came close. May I be attuned to your presence, Jesus, that I stop to allow you to work. I thank you, Jesus, for the unexpected gifts you have given me.

My soul is exceeding sorrowful unto death:
tarry ye here, and watch.

—Mark 14:34

Growing older doesn't necessitate letting go of faith. Even though our bodies are getting older and our thinking may not be as sharp as it once was, God is still the same. We can always depend on him.

> Search the scriptures; for in them ye think
> ye have eternal life: and they are they which
> testify of me. And ye will not come to me, that
> ye might have life.
>
> —John 5:39-40

Lord, help me recover my lost self. I have been sad for so long that I cannot even begin to think about a good life. Help me to find acceptance. Help me cope with nightmares that threaten to begin my despair all over again. Give me the strength to get through each coming day a little more intact. Fill me with the hope of a new dawn that I may see the sunrise once again. Amen.

They on the rock are they, which, when they hear, receive the word with joy; and these have no root, which for a while believe, and in time of temptation fall away.

—Luke 8:13

Does your word fall on good soil when I hear it, Lord? Or does it fall on rocky ground? Please help me cultivate my faith, so that it does not wither in time of temptation. Let my joy in you remain sharp and fresh.

Behold, a sower went forth to sow; And
when he sowed, some seeds fell by the way side,
and the fowls came and devoured them up:
Some fell upon stony places, where they had
not much earth: and forthwith they sprung up,
because they had no deepness of earth: And
when the sun was up, they were scorched; and
because they had no root, they withered away.
And some fell among thorns; and the thorns
sprung up, and choked them: But other fell into
good ground, and brought forth fruit, some an
hundredfold, some sixtyfold, some thirtyfold.

—Matthew 13:3-8

No matter the difficult people who cross our paths, there
is goodness in this world. It is there because we are
surrounded by the goodness of God and his angels and
the goodness they help us cultivate in ourselves.

> **What things soever ye desire, when ye pray, believe that ye receive them, and ye shall have them.**
>
> —Mark 11:24

I pray today to have more faith in my own abilities. I sometimes sell myself short and don't go out on a limb, afraid to fail at something even if I really want to try it. I let doubt scare me away and talk myself out of things, sure I don't have what it takes to make them happen. Then I regret never having gone after my dreams or feeling accomplished. I know that you have faith in me, but how do I find that faith for myself? Help me to recognize my own worth and strength, and to see that I am far more capable than I imagine myself to be. Help me to reach above and beyond where I am to get to where I want to be and to feel happy and fulfilled again. Amen.

> Ye both know me, and ye know whence I am:
> and I am not come of myself, but he that sent me
> is true, whom ye know not. But I know him: for
> I am from him, and he hath sent me.
>
> —John 7:28-29

For God so loves us, his children, that he sent his heavenly son into the world to guide, protect, and inspire us. When we love and recognize Jesus, we also love and recognize God.

> He sent them to preach the kingdom of God,
> and to heal the sick. And he said unto them,
> Take nothing for your journey, neither staves,
> nor scrip, neither bread, neither money; neither
> have two coats apiece.
>
> —Luke 9:2-3

When we travel with God, we can travel lightly, knowing that our needs will be provided. When you send me out on a spiritual journey, Lord, let me be eager to go, heading on my way without expectation or reservation. Let me put my faith in you.

> Even the Son of man came not to be
> ministered unto, but to minister, and to give his
> life a ransom for many.
>
> —Mark 10:45

To serve means to assist or be of use. Serving is one of the reasons we are on this earth and the reason Jesus himself said he came to the earth. When we serve, we reach out to meet the needs of others; service is an outward sign that we belong to God and desire to do his will. True service is not about grudgingly doing for

others because of obligation, but an act that flows willingly, as a channel for God's love. True servants give not just with their hands, but with their hearts.

> I am the light of the world: he that followeth me shall not walk in darkness, but shall have the light of life.
>
> —John 8:12

Open the curtains and let God's light shine through the window to your soul.

Unto you it is given to know the mystery of the kingdom of God: but unto them that are without, all these things are done in parables: That seeing they may see, and not perceive; and hearing they may hear, and not understand; lest at any time they should be converted, and their sins should be forgiven them.

—Mark 4:11-12

I know that I am only human, and not meant to understand your mysterious ways. Please help me have a sense of peace, a sense of understanding that it all does make sense, and that everything happens for a reason, even if you are the only one who knows what that reason is. Help me feel more balance, harmony, and serenity even when I'm afraid and uncertain.

Woe unto you also, ye lawyers! for ye lade men with burdens grievous to be borne, and ye yourselves touch not the burdens with one of your fingers. Woe unto you! for ye build the sepulchres of the prophets, and your fathers killed them. Truly ye bear witness that ye allow the deeds of your fathers: for they indeed killed them, and ye build their sepulchres.

—Luke 11:46-48

Thank you, Jesus, for the power of your forgiveness. Please let me turn to you in repentance as soon as I've done something wrong, not allowing that sin of grievous burden to set and deepen and become habitual.

He said unto them, But whom say ye that I am? Peter answering said, The Christ of God.

—Luke 9:20

We weren't direct witnesses of Jesus's public ministry, death, and resurrection. But like the apostles, we are called to share the story of Jesus's saving message. Let us never forget that the mystery at the heart of our faith is meant to be shared with others.

> For judgment I am come into this world,
> that they which see not might see; and that they
> which see might be made blind.
>
> —John 9:39

The Bible instructs us to have two goals: Wisdom—knowing and doing right—and common sense. Wisdom is the ability to meet each situation with discernment and good judgment, whether in dealing with others, making choices, or dispensing justice. Wisdom involves using the knowledge we have to take the proper course of action—if we know and don't act, it is the same as not knowing at all. When we let Christ become the source of our wisdom, he will guide us in making wise decisions and acting on them.

Behold, I send the promise of my Father upon you: but tarry ye in the city of Jerusalem, until ye be endued with power from on high.

—Luke 24:49

Elsewhere, the Bible says that there is a time for everything. Here, Jesus tells his followers to share God's word—but to wait for the Spirit, first. God, sometimes it is my turn to share, and sometimes my turn to wait in silence. Please put words in my mouth when I am called to witness, but also help me discern when I am meant to wait in stillness.

I thank thee, O Father, Lord of heaven and earth, because thou hast hid these things from the wise and prudent, and hast revealed them unto babes. Even so, Father: for so it seemed good in thy sight. All things are delivered unto me of my Father: and no man knoweth the Son, but the Father; neither knoweth any man the Father, save the Son, and he to whomsoever the Son will reveal him.

—Matthew 11:25-27

Bless these children, God. Keep them growing in mind and body. Keep them ever moving and reaching out toward the objects of their curiosity. And may they find, in all their explorations, the one thing that holds it all together: your love.

> If a kingdom be divided against itself, that kingdom cannot stand. And if a house be divided against itself, that house cannot stand.
>
> —Mark 3:24-25

Lord, you know the worries that keep me awake some nights. Please deliver me from this fretfulness, and grant me a deep and true trust in you and your wisdom.

> **What manner of communications are these that ye have one to another, as ye walk, and are sad?**
>
> —Luke 24:17

Jesus spoke these words to the disciples on the road to Emmaus, when they did not yet recognize him. Sometimes even when we are seeking God, our thoughts seem muddled. We find it difficult to see Jesus present and active in our lives. He seems far away. When we talk to others about our faith, as the disciples spoke to one another, sometimes God's presence becomes clear. How many times, when we look back at confusing times with the benefit of hindsight, do we realize that God was with us!

Take heed what ye hear: with what measure
ye mete, it shall be measured to you:
and unto you that hear shall more be given. For
he that hath, to him shall be given:
and he that hath not, from him shall be taken
even that which he hath.

—Mark 4:24-25

Thanksgiving is almost here, and Advent and Christmas will follow! Lord, during this season let me stay focused on you. Let me be truly thankful for my blessings, and not so intent on throwing the perfect party or preparing the best meal that I forget to be kind to my family and friends. Thank you for the gifts of faith, family, and friends!

In the last day, that great day of the feast,
Jesus stood and cried, saying, If any man thirst,
let him come unto me, and drink. He that
believeth on me, as the scripture hath said, out
of his belly shall flow rivers of living water.

—John 7:37-38

Lord, how precious water is to us, and how parched and
desperate we are when it's in short supply. How grateful
we are that in you we have access to the living water that
will never run dry! Keep us mindful of that refreshing
supply today, Lord. Fill us up, for we are thirsty.

The sabbath was made for man, and not man
for the sabbath: Therefore the Son of man is
Lord also of the sabbath.

—Mark 2:27-28

Almighty God, the world is a fearsome place where
violence is glorified, disease is rampant, and young
children are victimized daily. I am afraid for my family,
but you are our refuge and strength, and we seek
protection under the shadow of your wings. Continue to
guard my loved ones, Lord of the sabbath: my husband,
my children, and all others so dear to me. Preserve
them from harm, guard them from the pain of sorrow

and suffering, and
bless them with good
health. In times of
trouble, arm us for
the battle and guide
us safely through it.
Our confidence is
with you.

> Let your loins be girded about, and your lights burning; And ye yourselves like unto men that wait for their lord, when he will return from the wedding; that when he cometh and knocketh, they may open unto him immediately.
>
> —Luke 12:35-36

I look around and see there is work to be done. Thank you for the gift of work to do. Guide my hands that they may help others. Guide my heart to see where there is need and how to respond to it. Guide my thoughts to know that even if I can only do a little, that is enough to make a difference.

Blessed are those servants, whom the lord when he cometh shall find watching: verily I say unto you, that he shall gird himself, and make them to sit down to meat, and will come forth and serve them. And if he shall come in the second watch, or come in the third watch, and find them so, blessed are those servants. And this know, that if the goodman of the house had known what hour the thief would come, he would have watched, and not have suffered his house to be broken through. Be ye therefore ready also: for the Son of man cometh at an hour when ye think not.

—Luke 12:37-40

Father, you call to us to turn our backs on sin and turn our faces toward you. You even promise to give us your own Spirit to strengthen us to walk in your ways. I praise you today for your tireless love and concern for all people and for reaching out to us with your message of salvation.

> That there be some of them that stand here,
> which shall not taste of death, till they have seen
> the kingdom of God come with power.
>
> —Mark 9:1

I am strong as an ox, brave as a lion, and bold as a steer. God's Spirit within gives me the strength to move mountains and the courage to go the distance when others have given up. I am powerful in his presence!

Verily, verily, I say unto you, He that believeth on me hath everlasting life. I am that bread of life. Your fathers did eat manna in the wilderness, and are dead. This is the bread which cometh down from heaven, that a man may eat thereof, and not die. I am the living bread which came down from heaven: if any man eat of this bread, he shall live for ever: and the bread that I will give is my flesh, which I will give for the life of the world.

—John 6:47-51

Guidance is there, but you must look with your heart. Let go of what the mind and ego see, for it is not the truth. Follow where your heart leads, for it is led by the Spirit of a loving and powerful God who wants what is best for you!

November 27

> Take no thought for your life, what ye shall eat; neither for the body, what ye shall put on. The life is more than meat, and the body is more than raiment. Consider the ravens: for they neither sow nor reap; which neither have storehouse nor barn; and God feedeth them: how much more are ye better than the fowls?
>
> —Luke 12:22-24

Lord, each day you furnish us with our daily bread. You feed and nourish us, yet often we neglect to acknowledge your gifts of food. Forgive us, Father, for our selfishness and our disregard for your faithful care. We know that prayer should be a necessary part of every meal. If, in our haste, we forget to thank you, Lord, remind us of our rudeness. Our meals are not complete until we thank the giver for his many gifts.

> **Seest thou these great buildings? there shall not be left one stone upon another, that shall not be thrown down.**
>
> **—Mark 13:2**

So much of the crippling weight we carry upon our shoulders can be alleviated by simply understanding that we don't have to carry the burden alone. God is always there, walking beside us, and ready to take the entire load from us should we only ask him to.

Then said he also to him that bade him, When thou makest a dinner or a supper, call not thy friends, nor thy brethren, neither thy kinsmen, nor thy rich neighbours; lest they also bid thee again, and a recompence be made thee. But when thou makest a feast, call the poor, the maimed, the lame, the blind: And thou shalt be blessed; for they cannot recompense thee: for thou shalt be recompensed at the resurrection of the just.

—Luke 14:12-14

Our joy in God's love increases when we share it with others around us.

I am the bread of life: he that cometh to me shall never hunger; and he that believeth on me shall never thirst.

—John 6:35

Let me wake up each morning determined to see your presence in my life. Let me focus throughout the day not on what I don't have, but the blessings you give me so abundantly. It's easy for me to become distracted from your presence during the course of the day—but when I look, I see your mercy and compassion at work in my life.

December

> **The Son of man is not come to destroy men's lives, but to save them.**
>
> —**Luke 9:56**

As we enter the month that leads to your birth, Jesus, let me open my heart to you as your mother did. Mary didn't know what would happen, but she chose to follow God's plan. What an amazing woman of faith! I see echoes of her faith in some of the people I know from church, wise men and women who have a sense of inner peace about them. I know I want to be like that: let me start by saying yes to your plan for me today.

December 2

Jesus looked round about, and saith unto his disciples, How hardly shall they that have riches enter into the kingdom of God! And the disciples were astonished at his words. But Jesus answereth again, and saith unto them, Children, how hard is it for them that trust in riches to enter into the kingdom of God! It is easier for a camel to go through the eye of a needle, than for a rich man to enter into the kingdom of God.

—Mark 10:23-25

I wish to extend my love, Lord. So give me hands quick to work on behalf of the weak. Cause my feet to move swiftly in aid of the needy. Let my mouth speak words of encouragement and new life. And give my heart an ever-deepening joy through it all.

All wept, and bewailed her: but he said,
Weep not; she is not dead, but sleepeth.

—Luke 8:52

When the loss of someone we dearly love brings a cold darkness to our lives, it seems that darkness will be forever with us and our hearts will never feel joy again. We believe then that night will never end and day will never come. Yet the darkness will leave and the night will end when we hold on to our Lord, for he will bring light back into our lives. And in that light, our hopes will be renewed and joy will again reside in our hearts.

December 4

It is more blessed to give than to receive.

—Acts 20:35

Those who consider ourselves the Lord's servants
sometimes have a hard time receiving from others.
Although Jesus said, "It is more blessed to give than
receive," this statement also says, "it is blessed to
receive."

> **Let her alone; why trouble ye her? she hath wrought a good work on me. For ye have the poor with you always, and whensoever ye will ye may do them good: but me ye have not always. She hath done what she could: she is come aforehand to anoint my body to the burying.**
>
> **—Mark 14:6-8**

We all have something to offer: time, money, expertise. God exhorts us to give generously; in his infinite wisdom, he understands that when we give, we're not just helping others (worthy in and of itself). But we also help ourselves. Studies have shown that generosity helps to manage personal stress, and have linked unselfishness and giving with a general sense of life satisfaction and a lower risk of early death. When we reach outside ourselves, we connect with others; God wants that connection, that sense of purpose and happiness, for each of us. Dear Lord, help us to connect with our best selves; help us to be generous givers.

When Jesus knew in himself that his disciples murmured at it, he said unto them, Doth this offend you? What and if ye shall see the Son of man ascend up where he was before? It is the spirit that quickeneth; the flesh profiteth nothing: the words that I speak unto you, they are spirit, and they are life. But there are some of you that believe not. For Jesus knew from the beginning who they were that believed not, and who should betray him. And he said, Therefore said I unto you, that no man can come unto me, except it were given unto him of my Father.

—John 6:61-65

Your Word and your Scriptures give structure to my life. Sometimes I rebel against them, but I know that I am happier and have better relationships with others when I follow the path you have laid out for me.

Is a candle brought to be put under a bushel, or under a bed? and not to be set on a candlestick? For there is nothing hid, which shall not be manifested; neither was any thing kept secret, but that it should come abroad. If any man have ears to hear, let him hear.

—Mark 4:21-23

How can we recognize any of your needful ones we are to feed, clothe, and tend, Lord, when we see menace in every outstretched hand? Inspire and help us reclaim our world for living in, not hiding from. Amen.

December 8

The light of the body is the eye: therefore
when thine eye is single, thy whole body also is
full of light; but when thine eye is evil, thy body
also is full of darkness.

—Luke 11:34

In my choice of friends, in my choice of entertainment,
in my choice of work, let me seek out the holy and
look towards the light.

> Go ye into all the world, and preach the
> gospel to every creature.
>
> —Mark 16:15

Shopping, wrapping, traveling, cooking. So much to do
this season as we hurry toward the manger, answering
God's call as did those folk so long ago, to go, believe,
and do. Practice the notes of the carol, for soon it will
be time to sing out "Gloria!" at what we'll see and hear.

> I am the good shepherd, and know my sheep,
> and am known of mine. As the Father knoweth
> me, even so know I the Father: and I lay down
> my life for the sheep.
>
> —John 10:14-15

Lord, my heart is uplifted as I think of the special gift you have given me: a community of faith. I thank you for my church and for the dear people who have become part of my support system. I thank you for your invitation to spend time with you. My husband and children and I need the blessings of church attendance. We need the fellowship and care of other believers; we need to be refreshed with the words of Scripture and feel the power of prayer washing over us. We need to experience your presence, Lord, in your house, and to become involved in your work. Please continue to strengthen our children's ties to your church so that they, too, may participate in the joys of life in the Christian community.

And other sheep I have, which are not of this fold: them also I must bring, and they shall hear my voice; and there shall be one fold, and one shepherd. Therefore doth my Father love me, because I lay down my life, that I might take it again.

—John 10:16-17

Opposites don't attract nearly as often as they repel, if we are to believe the headlines. Pick a race, color, creed, or lifestyle, Lord of all, and we'll find something to fight about. Deliver us from stereotypes. Inspire us to spot value in everyone we meet. As we dodge the curses and hatred, we are relieved there is room for all of us beneath your wings. Bless our diversity; may it flourish.

The children of this world marry, and are given in marriage: But they which shall be accounted worthy to obtain that world, and the resurrection from the dead, neither marry, nor are given in marriage: Neither can they die any more: for they are equal unto the angels; and are the children of God, being the children of the resurrection.

—Luke 20:34-36

Sometimes the circumstances of our lives are so difficult, Lord! Often misfortunes seem to come all at once. Other times ongoing, wear-me-down situations or relationships seem to follow us day in and day out. A life of faith is not defined by these things—but it is not exempt, either. Suffering is as real for the faithful as for anyone else. However, we have an eternal comfort and hope that lifts us up. In that comfort and hope, God carries us, heals us with the balm of his tender mercies, and strengthens us to carry on in what is good.

> **Heaven and earth shall pass away: but my words shall not pass away.**
>
> **—Mark 13:31**

We are far too easily pleased, Lord. We pursue every form of recreation, as if it could somehow save us. We involve ourselves in relationship after relationship, hoping that each new conquest will give us full satisfaction. We work and work, earning more and more money, thinking that somehow happiness can be bought, or that the joy of the future can be mortgaged today. Yes, we are far too easily pleased with all we can do for ourselves. But how much energy would we exert toward obtaining our true home if we could

only see the place you've prepared for us? Give us that vision, God, and the determination to reach for your promises every day.

Fear not; I am the first and the last: I am he
that liveth, and was dead; and, behold, I am
alive for evermore.

—**Revelation 1:17-18**

When we grieve for lost loved ones, we grieve for
ourselves. Let us celebrate that those who have gone
home to heaven now know the full essence of God's
true love.

Suppose ye that I am come to give peace on earth? I tell you, Nay; but rather division: For from henceforth there shall be five in one house divided, three against two, and two against three. The father shall be divided against the son, and the son against the father; the mother against the daughter, and the daughter against the mother; the mother in law against her daughter in law, and the daughter in law against her mother in law.

—Luke 12:51-53

Guide my quarrelsome, divided family to common ground, God of reconciliation; mediate our negotiations; inspire solutions. Faith in a wise and trustworthy God, even in broken times like these, divides our troubles and multiplies unfathomable possibilities for renewed life.

If any man shall say to you, Lo, here is Christ; or, lo, he is there; believe him not: For false Christs and false prophets shall rise, and shall shew signs and wonders, to seduce, if it were possible, even the elect. But take ye heed: behold, I have foretold you all things.

—Mark 13:21-23

Truth is a narrow road, and it's easy to fall to one side or the other. For every beautiful kernel of truth, there are a thousand lies that can be made around it. Staying on the straight-and-narrow would be impossible if it weren't for the Spirit of God, who leads us to all truth. Delving into God's Word with the Holy Spirit to guide us is the best way to stay on track and keep walking in the truth.

Go your way, and tell John what things ye
have seen and heard; how that the blind see,
the lame walk, the lepers are cleansed, the deaf
hear, the dead are raised, to the poor the gospel
is preached. And blessed is he, whosoever shall
not be offended in me.

—Luke 7:22-23

Our eternal blessing is Jesus our Savior. God, when I'm
feeling down about myself and my purpose in life, may
I remember to glorify you—that is my purpose!

If I do not the works of my Father, believe
me not. But if I do, though ye believe not
me, believe the works: that ye may know, and
believe, that the Father is in me, and I in him.

—John 10:37-38

We spend so much time shopping and decorating! It seems small, but God, please do help me choose good gifts for my family and friends, thoughtful ones that express my love for them. But please also don't let my ego get wrapped up in it, forgetting that the connection

we share is more important than any individual gift. Let me stay focused on love this season, as always: your love for us, our love for you, and our love for each other.

But take heed to yourselves: for they
shall deliver you up to councils; and in the
synagogues ye shall be beaten: and ye shall be
brought before rulers and kings for my sake, for
a testimony against them. And the gospel must
first be published among all nations.

—Mark 13:9-10

It is easy to have faith when things are going well, when the bills are paid and everyone is happy and in good health. But blessed is the person who has steadfast and unmoving faith when everything is going wrong. That's when faith is most needed—and least employed. If a person can suspend all intellectual judgment, look beyond the illusion of negative appearances, and believe in a Higher Power at work behind the scenes, faith will begin to move mountains, and positive solutions will appear. By putting the mighty power to work, faith will begin to work some mighty powerful miracles in your life.

> Be not afraid of them that kill the body, and after that have no more that they can do. But I will forewarn you whom ye shall fear: Fear him, which after he hath killed hath power to cast into hell; yea, I say unto you, Fear him.
>
> —Luke 12:4-5

I come to you today humbled and grateful for the powerful healing you have given me. I was so ill and broken, and weak in body and spirit, and I was losing my faith that I would ever feel good again. Yet you took care of me. Your love provided me with all the medicine I could ever need, and the hope of your eternal presence motivated me to stay in faith, even when things seemed so bleak. I thank you from the bottom of my heart for this new sense of well-being and health, and for knowing that if I stay positive and hopeful, your loving will for me will prevail over any disease or challenge. Amen.

> While ye have light, believe in the light, that
> ye may be the children of light.
>
> —John 12:36

God promises us his comfort, but he also uses us as his agents to comfort others. In fact, the difficulties we've gone through often give us the ability to reassure others who are now going through the same experiences. How will God use you to extend comfort to someone else?

> There shall be weeping and gnashing of teeth, when ye shall see Abraham, and Isaac, and Jacob, and all the prophets, in the kingdom of God, and you yourselves thrust out. And they shall come from the east, and from the west, and from the north, and from the south, and shall sit down in the kingdom of God. And, behold, there are last which shall be first, and there are first which shall be last.
>
> —Luke 13:28-30

Lord, sometimes I resist your grace. It's not that I don't want to be closer to you, but I know I don't deserve it. I stew over my past sins, wallowing in guilt. I don't want to take your forgiveness for granted, but neither do I want to forget that you are always reaching out to me, ready to draw me back to you.

Is it not written, My house shall be called
of all nations the house of prayer? but ye have
made it a den of thieves.

—Mark 11:17

We all prefer to deal with honest people—people we
can trust—people who will not lie or try to deceive us.
A noble goal for one's life is to pursue honesty—honesty
with others, with ourselves, and with God. Yet it is not
natural to tell the truth. Honesty can seem to leave us
open to attack—to tear down the walls of protection we
would rather erect in our lives. Scripture tells us, "The
truth shall make you free." Although it might be hard to
be honest, if we do it with loving intentions, the burden
that dishonesty brings will be lifted.

> **The kingdom of God is come nigh unto you.**
>
> —Luke 10:9

The Christmas tree, O God, is groaning beneath gift-wrapped anticipation. The table spread before us is resplendent with shared foods prepared by loving hands, for which we give thanks. And now, as this waiting season ticks to a bell-ringing, midnight-marvelous close, we around this table are scooting over to make room for the anticipated guest. Come, blessing us with the gift of your presence as we say, "Welcome."

For God so loved the world, that he gave his only begotten Son, that whosoever believeth in him should not perish, but have everlasting life. For God sent not his Son into the world to condemn the world; but that the world through him might be saved. He that believeth on him is not condemned: but he that believeth not is condemned already, because he hath not believed in the name of the only begotten Son of God.

—John 3:16-18

Compassionate and holy God, we celebrate your coming into this world. We celebrate with hope, we celebrate with peace, we celebrate with joy. Through your giving our lives are secure. Through your love we, too, can give love. You are the source of our being. Joy to our world.

> **I Jesus have sent mine angel to testify unto you these things in the churches. I am the root and the offspring of David, and the bright and morning star.**
>
> **—Revelation 22:16**

We teach children that the sun, the moon, and the stars are always in the sky, even when we cannot see them. Let me trust, Lord, that even when I don't perceive you working in my life, you are still present!

> **Jesus beholding him loved him, and said unto him, One thing thou lackest: go thy way, sell whatsoever thou hast, and give to the poor, and thou shalt have treasure in heaven: and come, take up the cross, and follow me.**
>
> **—Mark 10:21**

Jesus, I ask you to please keep drawing me into a closer relationship with you. Sometimes I think of my good acts like a running tally: letting someone in ahead of me in traffic gets me a point, donating money to someone in need gets me ten. But that's a small,

legalistic way of thinking. Let me do good things not in hope of a reward but simply to pass along the tremendous grace you have granted to me.

Then said Jesus to them again, Peace be unto you: as my Father hath sent me, even so send I you. And when he had said this, he breathed on them, and saith unto them, Receive ye the Holy Ghost.

—John 20:21-22

The days after Christmas can sometimes be a bit of a letdown, but they can be peaceful, too. After all the preparation and rush, we have a little time to reflect and talk. Things that weren't "important" enough to get brought up at the big family meals make their way into conversation. Let me be grateful, Lord, for these gentle times of relaxation and renewal as we prepare for the end of the year.

The Spirit of the Lord is upon me, because he hath anointed me to preach the gospel to the poor; he hath sent me to heal the brokenhearted, to preach deliverance to the captives, and recovering of sight to the blind, to set at liberty them that are bruised, to preach the acceptable year of the Lord.

—Luke 4:18-19

The people I know who walk in the ways of God are savory with the fruit of God's Spirit; they're the kind of people I can't be around enough. Their kind and gentle ways radiate peace. Their joy is contagious. Their faithfulness is inspiring. So many things about them make me want to be more like them—and more like Christ.

> **It is done. I am Alpha and Omega, the beginning and the end.**
>
> **—Revelation 21:6**

Loving God, help us sense your angelic messengers whenever and wherever and however they come to us. In the darkness of winter, the brightness of spring, the abundance of summer, the transitions of autumn, may we expect to be visited by your heavenly beings. And when those visits happen, may our eyes be open and our gratitude heartfelt.

I am the way, the truth, and the life: no man cometh unto the Father, but by me. If ye had known me, ye should have known my Father also: and from henceforth ye know him, and have seen him.

—John 14:6-7

Life becomes much easier and more enjoyable when we know we are never alone. We always have our Higher Power to turn to for strength, hope, guidance, and renewal. God is on the job 24 hours a day, 7 days a week, and 365 days a year.